KANSAS CITY COMEDY

The Unbelievable True Story of Stanford & Sons, Its Outlaw Owners and the Most Infamous Stand-Up Sets of All Time

MIKE BRIDENSTINE

Published by The History Press
An imprint of Arcadia Publishing
Charleston, SC
www.historypress.com

Cover art courtesy of Greg Edwards and Jake Lloyd Bacon.

First published 2025

Manufactured in the United States

ISBN 9781467170161

Library of Congress Control Number: 2025943127

"The comedy business is full of liars, psychos, and totally unsavory characters. But none of them compare to the absolute debauchery of Stanford & Sons in KC. It was like if San Quentin had an open mic. Mike Bridenstine brilliantly tells the many outrageous tales of this almost too-crazy-to-believe place that will never happen anywhere again."
—Tom Segura

"There's two good reasons to read a great book. One of them is pure enjoyment. The other is so you can boast to your mates about it. When you read about the insane events that went down at these infamous stand-up routines, you'll be telling everyone you know. A hilarious, inspired read from a writer who truly understands the machinations of comedy."
—Eran Creevy

"I only had a brief email exchange with one of the owners of Stanford & Sons and it was more than enough for me to believe every bit of tasteless skullduggery attributed to them. An excellent read for anyone interested in stand-up lore."
—Kyle Kinane

"Mike is an incredible, important historian of the pre–vertical video world of comedy and its important, often ridiculous, oral history and lore. The first time I ever performed at Stanford & Sons in my hometown of KC, Craig Glazer tried to sell me his book instead of paying me for a feature weekend and said he'd even throw in 'some other good stuff.' I have a few guesses as to what the 'good stuff' was, and I'd gladly do the same exchange for any of Mike's writings, including this well-thought-out time capsule of an infamous set and the bizarre world that fostered it."
—Kyle Ayers

"When I moved to Kansas City in 2007, I heard about these stories, and it was great to finally read what actually happened. Mike is a amazing storyteller."
—Brooks Wheelan

CONTENTS

FOREWORD

Stand-up comedy was at its lowest in the late '90s. The Comedy Boom of the '80s had long been over, and the vast stand-up scene we know today wouldn't appear for at least another twenty years. Comedy clubs were closing more often than they were opening. Of course, you could go to L.A. or New York and have a chance at fame, but in the Midwest we were just trying to get better at this thing we loved so much. This was before Instagram and TikTok, where you could make a name for yourself in the confines of your own safe space. If you were a comic and wanted to get booked in Omaha, you drove your ass up to Omaha on their open mic night and hoped the booker was there, or that you did so well that someone told them about you. And if you were a patron? Good luck, cause who knows what kind of show you could walk into back then—hacky guitar acts, cruise ship impressionists and celebrities you thought you'd forgotten about littered the lineups. Did you know there was a Gallagher II? Or that Skippy from *Family Ties* does comedy? Did you know Jeff Dunham talks to his puppets when they are not on stage? Obviously, Mr. Dunham is doing very well nowadays. But I feel like people need to know that he does that.

It may seem odd that in the middle of comedy's darkest hour, a comedy scene would emerge in the "Paris of the Plains," but it did. Fueled by a mix of upcoming talent, road-weary veterans, local crazies, delusion, alcohol and myriad other substances, the KC comedy scene thrived for a few years as a true community, thanks in large part to people like Emery Emery, Joe Caronia and other names that may not mean much to anyone who wasn't there. And all of it happened under the roof of one of the most notorious clubs to ever exist, Stanford & Sons in Westport. The owners may have been drug-addict recreational gangsters, but they also allowed you to do what you wanted as long as…well, you'll find out in this book just where their limits were.

I loved Stanford's in Westport. It was my clubhouse. The comedy club itself was perfect. Low ceilings, not too deep and the crowds were always great. I would walk in and hand my coat to the bartender with sixty dollars in the front pocket, go upstairs and do my set, and when I left, I would get my coat with a brand-new bag of weed where the money once was. It was a young comic's paradise. This book is a great look into that scene and that club and its owners, the Glazer brothers. It's a time I have never forgotten, and I look back at it fondly.

Chris Porter. *Greg Edwards.*

The thing about being part of a "scene" is that you don't know you're in one when it's happening. I doubt people were at Studio 54 in the '70s like, "Oh, man, they are totally gonna do several documentaries about all the drugs and illicit sex we're having!" No, they were just doing the drugs and the sex. And eventually the money laundering. My point is, as participants, we didn't think we were a scene. We were just comics trying to be comics at a time when that wasn't even considered possible by most.

I'm so happy you've chosen to read this book. Mike really did a great job. It's an amazing look into an incredible time of my life, and I hope you enjoy reading about it as much as I did experiencing it.

"Think about it!"[1]

—CHRIS PORTER, 2024

PROLOGUE

It all started with a dead 'possum, but it escalated quickly from there. That statement is as true for the infamous open mic story I'm going to tell you later as it is for me and the writing of this book. Especially since I didn't know this was even going to be a book when I started. What I had initially hoped it would be was an article I could pitch somewhere like *Vulture* or whoever else was accepting niche histories about comedy weirdos. But what I ended up with was more than thirty-five thousand words of text and the most fun I've had writing anything in my life.

To be fair, I didn't know that my first book, *The Perfect Amount of Wrong*, was going to be a book either. I guess I'm just a sucker for bizarre comedy stories. And so I kept following this particular bizarre comedy story to see where it would lead. And where it led was inside the amazing world of the Kansas City comedy scene, which included some of the most unreal characters I've ever come across. It took me to the birth of the Comedy Boom in the Midwest and even to the doorstep of the movie industry. Or at least inside a few current (and not so current) headlines from the Hollywood trades. And at the end of this journey, I also believe I've been led to the conclusion that Kansas City, as it pertains to the history of American comedy, deserves a prominent seat at the table.

Consistently, throughout writing this book, I was also confronted by bizarre coincidences, as if the universe itself were telling me to go deeper down this rabbit hole—or, I guess, 'possum hole. For starters, two days after I finished listening to *The King of Sting*, an obscure sixteen-year-old memoir written by the owner of a comedy club in Kansas City (a book that was free on Audible), I happened to see an article in *Deadline* announcing that that very book was going to become a movie. The timing on that was crazy enough. But then when I talked to Eran Creevy, the writer/director of the movie, shortly after, he told me about a specific 2013 article from the *Kansas City Pitch* that he thought would perfectly ground the movie in modern day. And when I found that equally obscure, eleven-year-old article from a local Kansas City publication, one of the specific scenes Creevy had told me about featured Nick Vatterott, a comedian friend of mine for more than twenty years and a prominent subject of my last book about the Chicago stand-up scene. So I decided to take the hint—this had to be a book.

Besides Vatterott, plenty of other unlikely names from my comedy past began to resurface as well. As of 2025, I've done stand-up comedy for twenty-three years. But the more I wrote about and researched the Kansas City scene, the more I kept being drawn back to year one of my career. That's when I was a fifth-year senior at the University of Iowa hosting a comedy night at a campus bar called the Summit. In *The Perfect Amount of Wrong*, I said the Summit mostly featured hack road comics with dated acts. Which is true. But there were also some who were great. And there were exactly five times when a headliner at the Summit was so good they got a standing ovation, at least while I was present. And I still remember all their names: Troy Baxley, Full Contact (the duo of Bob Jay and Tim Kaminski), Bengt Washburn, Chris "Crazy Legs" Fonseca and Steve Kramer. Those were the guys who blew the fucking roof off the place.

In the two decades since my time at the Summit, I've run into only one of those guys (Troy Baxley, one time, when I featured for Bert Kreischer at the Denver Improv in 2012). But while I was writing this book, I immediately realized that Steve Kramer was a pretty major figure in the Kansas City story. Then Chris "Crazy Legs" Fonseca—and more specifically his standing ovations—also turned up in a side story about comedian Emery Emery. And it all served to remind me that Iowa City is probably where my interest in infamous sets started in the first place. And I'll tell you about that soon enough.

As I did research for this book, I kept asking myself what the most infamous set in the history of comedy might actually be, and that also got oddly personal. A little later in the book, I'll be declaring one specific set "the most infamous open mic set of all time." But I wondered how much I needed to qualify that statement. I mean, throughout the history of stand-up, there are several "most infamous set of all time" candidates worth discussing. There's

Michael Richards's racist tirade at the Laugh Factory in Hollywood in 2006, which was also the first time I'd ever heard of TMZ, as well as the first example of a crowd work video going viral. There's also guitar comic Kenny Moore, who once dealt with a heckler by going full "Honky Tonk Man" on his ass and smashing a guitar over the guy's head in 1989 or '90.[2] Maybe the incident happened at Jodie's Comedy Shop in Bossier City, Louisiana, or maybe nobody knows for sure anymore where it happened.

But both of those sets have obvious problems with their candidacies. For one, they were joyless. In each grainy clip, the crowd unanimously turned on the comedian. In both cases, someone shouted that the man's behavior was either "unnecessary" or "uncalled for" before both comics just kind of left the stage in shame while the audiences headed for the exits. When Richards appeared live via satellite on the *Late Show with David Letterman* three days later to apologize for his "trash talk" to "some Afro-Americans," Jerry Seinfeld had to tell the live audience to "stop laughing" because "it's not funny." And honestly, where's the fun in *that*?

Alternatively, the most infamous set of all time might be Chris Rock and "the Slap" from the Academy Awards in 2022. But that one has more to do with the bad behavior of one bizarre audience member than it does with the set itself. There's a huge difference between what Richards let fly and what Rock said ("*G.I. Jane 2*—can't wait to see it!") to a humorless celebrity. I'm not even sure I'd call what Rock did that night "stand-up" or just another celebrity introducing the nominees for Best Documentary Feature off a teleprompter and doing one regrettable riff.

And while Rock may have gotten the shit slapped out of him that night in 2022, throughout history several comedians have actually died onstage or directly after their performances. Some on stages and in situations not too dissimilar from the Academy Awards. That includes Welsh comedian Tommy Cooper,[3] who is said to have died in front of 12 million viewers[4] live on British public television in 1984. And it includes Harry Einstein (aka Parkyakarkus), the father of comedians Albert Brooks and Bob Einstein, who died immediately following a performance at the Friars Club roast of Lucille Ball and Desi Arnaz in 1958.

Even longer ago, though geographically closer to our story, vaudeville comedian Walter S. "Rube" Dickinson performed at the grand opening of Kansas City's second Orpheum Theater in late December 1914, only to have his skull crushed while standing in front of it the next day.[5] Apparently, a horse-drawn delivery wagon backed into a post at the Muehlbach Hotel next door,[6] bringing down a 250-foot wooden canopy and killing Dickinson

The Orpheum Theater. *Missouri Valley Special Collections.*

along with two other men. That's not necessarily how you want to *open a theater*. But again, I don't know if these events qualify as the most infamous sets either. Death is not performance, after all. Death is death.

There are a handful of other historically significant performances that would definitely qualify as "infamous." Usually sets like these are performed by an all-time great like Lenny Bruce, George Carlin or Richard Pryor. And then that set is said to have paved the way for the entirety of comedy that would follow. While the actual significance of those sets can't really be overstated, nobody would really bat an eye in modern times if they heard a comic say "schmuck" onstage at a club like they did in the times Bruce said and was then arrested for saying them. Or as his mother, Sally Marr, told *Playboy*[7] in 1989, "Lenny lived so that old ladies today can talk like he talked."

The scenario is probably also true for an infamous Pryor set from 1967 at the Aladdin hotel and casino in Las Vegas. Feeling like a phony for trying to appeal to white tourists, Pryor started to rebel by saying words like *damn* and *shit* in his act. That alone got him repeated warnings[8] from Aladdin entertainment director Dick Kanellis. Eventually, Pryor decided one night that he'd had enough and reportedly asked the crowd, "What the fuck am I doing here?" before leaving the stage. From there, the legend goes, the young Richard Pryor decided to become *Richard Motherfucking Pryor*, the greatest comic to ever do it. It's as ingrained in the lore of stand-up as Robert Johnson

Connie Francis and Richard Kanellis. *Kanellis family collection.*

selling his soul to the devil at the crossroads is to the history of rock-and-roll. But again, I don't know who would find what Pryor said offensive at any club in America today. But what kind of trailblazer would he be if they did?

Besides its historical significance, the Pryor story has personal significance for me since Dick Kanellis happens to be my great-uncle. Granted, I never met the guy—he died six years before I was born. And I had no idea that

Richard Kanellis; Connie Francis; and Richard's mother, Elda, and sister, Athena Jean. *Kanellis family collection.*

my maternal grandfather's younger brother was even involved in comedy until I watched the 2013 documentary *Richard Pryor: Omit the Logic* and his name was mentioned. In fact, my own family lore about Uncle Dick was just that he'd been married to singer Connie Francis for all of four months in 1964. But while I was researching this book, I learned that he was also a judge for the 1961 Vegas bout between Cassius Clay (the future Muhammad Ali) and Duke Sabedong—the same fight for which the nineteen-year-old Clay appeared on a radio show with professional wrestler Gorgeous George, which made Clay decide to adopt his brash trash-talking ways for the rest of his career.[9] It was a fight already known to me as a fan of Ali's and of professional wrestling. Just not as a great-nephew. I digress, but I told you this was personal.

For a stand-up performance to truly be the infamy GOAT (the greatest of all time) or the Muhammad Ali of bad sets, it can't boast only negative interactions with audience members. Nor hinge on an act of God. It should be intentional and pre-planned. And it can't be joyless. In fact, ideally, the performance should probably divide the audience. Or at least have a small contingent of support while the performance is happening, even though a majority of the audience probably wants the performer dead. And besides all that, the set should stand the test of time. Unfortunately, Lenny Bruce saying "tuchus" and other adorable Yiddish phrases at the Troubadour in 1962, or George Carlin saying the "Seven Words You Can Never Say on Television" in Milwaukee in 1972, won't cut it in this context. So the set might have to be way more recent.

Fortunately, there are a number of stories that do fit this description. I even shared a few in my previous book. And while there's no way I've heard every infamous comedy story in recent history, I can say that of the stories I *have* heard about these types of sets, there are three that stand apart. At least to me. And two of those sets just so happen to have taken place in Kansas City in the early 2000s. They became the impetus for this book.

The third story, which predates the other two, has great personal significance to me. And it's a story that takes place in Iowa City, where my career began. It also happens to be the first live stand-up set I ever saw in my life. And it will also serve as a starting place for this book. I consider it my origin story.

Introduction

NORM MACDONALD AT HANCHER AUDITORIUM, 1997

"They're gonna hate me."

Norm Macdonald was pacing nervously backstage[10] before his set at old Hancher Auditorium in Iowa City on June 22, 1997. About 1,300 people[11] had come that night to see Macdonald, along with his *Saturday Night Live* cast mates Jim Breuer and Darrell Hammond, perform as part of a fundraiser for the University of Iowa Athletic Department. Apparently, Macdonald had reason to be nervous, even after that night's host insisted that the crowd would love him.

"No," Norm assured him. "They'll hate me."

As it turned out, Norm was right. The crowd, or a vast majority of the people in it, did indeed hate him that night. And in the decades since, his set has become either legendary or a despicable tragedy, depending on who you ask. When the *Cedar Rapids Gazette* did a twenty-year anniversary article about the performance titled "The Night Norm Macdonald Mortified the University of Iowa," some attendees were *still* acting as if his comedy set was the worst thing to ever happen to the good people of Eastern Iowa. "They revisited it like it was a war," comedian Tom Segura laughed when we talked about it on my podcast in 2019. "Because of you, this became my favorite story ever."

Norm was the night's headliner. But the first act introduced by the host wasn't actually a stand-up at all. It was local improv troupe ComedySportz of the Quad Cities. And while they're largely forgotten in the retellings of this story, their inclusion in the show might actually be the catalyst, or at least *a* catalyst, for what came later.

Norm Macdonald walks the crowd at Hancher. Painting by Nicholas Knudson. *Author's collection.*

As former Cedar Rapids comedy club owner Jeff Johnson told me, "I did not book Norm or Jim Breuer or Darrell Hammond. However, I did book the improv group that opened for them. And I told [the university's event organizers] numerous times it was a mistake. It should have been: no improv group, Darrell does 30, Breuer does 30, Norm does 45, and you got a great show. And I really don't believe that it would have turned into what it turned into."

Comedy shows can drag after the ninety-minute mark. And as a longtime producer, Johnson knew that an extended set by ComedySportz meant the night would run long. But it wasn't just an extended set. "They did *forty-five minutes*," Johnson remembered.[12] "Which is stupid. That's what set the tone of the whole night."

As the improv set dragged on, Johnson headed backstage to see if there was any way he could cut the performance short. And he remembers frustration from the *SNL* stars as they decided what would happen next. "They're like, 'Okay, who's going up now?'" Johnson said. "And Hammond was like, 'I'm going up.' And then, of course, he does a pretty long set. And then Breuer does a long set. And Norm was just getting madder and madder. He's like, 'How long does this show last?' He's just pissed. [The show] was set up for failure. And by the time Norm got up, it was too late."

Darrell Hammond, at the time, was best known for his impression of President Bill Clinton. But in the lead-up to the event, the *Iowa City Press-Citizen* reminded readers that Hammond's "claims to fame" also included an impersonation of Reverend Jesse Jackson.[13] Hammond, in case you needed a reminder, is white. Jackson—the politician, civil rights activist and protégé of Martin Luther King—is pretty famously Black. And when Hammond did that impression on TV, they would darken his skin. But since none of the previews or reviews of the event mentioned it, I'm not sure if that impression was performed, or if it even would have registered as anything but innocent fun to a predominantly white crowd in Iowa in 1990s—and, to be fair, my teenage self included. Times do indeed change. So Hammond was likely not considered very offensive.

Jim Breuer, however—probably most famous at the time for his "Goat Boy" character—went up after Hammond and got a little more risqué, with jokes about alcohol and marijuana. One of the bits he told that night was a guide on how to avoid getting sick from drinking. And to do this, he created an analogy where a stomach acted like a bouncer at a house party. Then he began to personify the different types of alcohol one could drink at this party by doing accents based on the regions from which the liquor comes. The Beck's beer character got a German accent complete with a Nazi salute, the scotch character got a Scottish accent and bagpipes, the sake character was a Japanese tourist who spoke in pidgin English. And for tequila, he did multiple stereotypical Latino accents, said that tequila "sneak[s] into the party when nobody's looking" and then had one of the tequila characters shoot a gun into the air until the bouncer—a stomach—kicked everyone out by vomiting.

"I remember thinking that even *he* was pushing it a bit," said one attendee in an anniversary article, referring just to the drug and alcohol references, not even the ethnic accents or racial stereotypes. And still, none of that registered as overly offensive to anyone in the papers in the days after the event.

It was Macdonald alone they hated. And Macdonald alone who terrorized the all-ages crowd until they fled into the aisles.

It was all supposed to go so much differently. For years—according to Mike Hlas of the *Gazette*—the AEGON Advantage Golf Tournament had raised money for the University of Iowa Athletics Hall of Fame and the renovation of the university's golf course. This year, the idea was that in addition to the golf tournament, participants would be treated to a night of entertainment—some light, family-friendly guffaws the night before the main event. And while the comedy show was open to the public, half or more of the crowd (anywhere from 650 to 780 people) were also registered for, or associated with, the tournament. Those people did not get what they thought they were going to get. "It was sick," an angry golfer from Davenport told the *Iowa City Press-Citizen* soon after, "absolutely sick."[14]

According to the University of Iowa's athletic director at the time, Bob Bowlsby, the department had made it crystal clear to the booking agents that they wanted "G-rated" comedy from the performers.[15] And according to department spokesman Rick Klatt, the university was assured that Macdonald could meet those guidelines.[16] "We were very explicit about the details of the event," Klatt said, "and about the type of people who would be there."

"The University of Iowa had taken the time to put into the contract of each of the three to make it clear there would be kids there (and adjust their content accordingly)," AEGON's chief operating officer Pat Baird told the *Gazette* in 2017. "Two of the three lived up to that and one did not."

"You had Norm Macdonald," Johnson, a more experienced booker, told me in 2024. "You have to know what you're getting there—the guy who did eighty million OJ jokes. That's what you're gonna get. You're gonna get inappropriate stuff. Just because you want *SNL* doesn't mean you book Norm."

At the time, I was a seventeen-year-old about to enter my senior year at Muscatine High School, which was just under an hour away. So you could technically count me as one of the children in attendance. I was a huge fan of Macdonald's from *SNL*. And I was accompanied to the show that night by a few of my high school friends, as well as my overprotective mother, who drove us all there. And while I've seen thousands of live stand-up shows since, this is still the most famous—or most infamous—of all the shows I've seen. I guess I peaked early. Fortunately, the show did not.

In Breuer's version[17] of that night's events (as told onstage at the Funny Bone in Des Moines in 2010), "They go, 'Ladies and gentlemen, your headliner, Mr. Norm Macdonald!' And like, I can't wait to watch this guy rip the place—and the place goes *nuts* [makes the sound of a crowd roaring]. Little kids [makes the sound of kids cheering]. And I am not exaggerating—I'm gonna make this as G-rated as possible—Norm gets to the podium and he goes [in a perfect Norm impression], 'Ahhh, let me ask you something:

If you're a gay guy, why would you want to be the *ass* guy? What advantage is it if you're gay and you're like, Hey, can I be the ass guy? It's gonna hurt. This thing is just ripping into you.'" And then Breuer reenacted his own backstage look of shock at the material from 1997 as the 2010 crowd in Des Moines roared at how hilariously inappropriate Norm's material was for an audience filled with families and children. And that's the most "G-rated as possible" version of the joke.

A recording[18] of the actual version, which I found on YouTube from a different Norm performance, would have been more along the lines of, "One thing I realize about gay guys is one of them gets gypped. You know—when there's two gay guys? That's for goddamned sure. One of those guys is having a grand old time. The other guy? Man, he got the raw end of that deal. I don't know how they figure it out, man. But one guy gets to use his *cock*. That's a huge advantage in a relationship. One guys says, 'Hey, I'll tell you what, man. I'll use my cock. How 'bout you use the *inside of your ass*?' The other guy's like, 'I'm not sure that's fair, man. Are you sure this will be as fun for each of us, dude?'"

And that's how Macdonald *opened* his set at Hancher that night, for an all-ages show. "When Norm took the stage," remembered an Iowa City resident in the anniversary article, "he immediately launched into a bit that was intentionally supposed to be offensive to most of the audience. As it went on, people got up and left in large numbers."

"People are leaving in packs of thirties and forties," Breuer added, "like a fire broke out. 'Take the children and let's run!'"

And when Macdonald noticed people were leaving, he stopped and asked them, "What do you want to talk about—losing your luggage at the airport?"

"Five or ten minutes later," another witness remembered, "he's telling the pig joke."

"That's the one thing I remember," Johnson told me. "That pig joke. And that just sums it all up."

The pig joke, I should warn you, is not for the faint of heart. But it also happens to be the only joke I remember clearly from Norm's set that night. Which also makes it the joke I've repeated every time I've retold this story since 1997. Most notably, I told it to Tom Segura and producer Brian Redban on episode 28 of the *Your Mom's House* podcast in 2011. Then a clip of that episode was included in the viral YouTube short "Norm Macdonald Had a Secret" by Styrofoam Bonfire in 2022. Which means millions of people have heard my version of the story. The only thing is, after doing some research on the set, I don't think I've been telling the pig bit accurately all these years.

As it turns out, Macdonald discussed the joke on Comedy Central's *Turn Ben Stein On* in 2001. And the aforementioned YouTube audio of his set also included the joke. So I think it's safe to say, officially this time, the pig joke would have probably gone something like this: "I like some pornography. Sometimes I just get so repelled by it. You ever have those friends of yours go, 'Hey man, I got a video of a guy fucking a pig?' I didn't even think that was real—bestiality. That's what they call it—bestiality. That's a real thing, man. I never heard of a dude doing that. And I know a lot of people, man. None of them, to my knowledge, have ever fucked an animal. I never even heard a guy who knew a guy. But I know that people fuck animals on account of they got that word, bestiality. That's not easy getting a fucking word. That's hard getting a word going. They had to have calls at the goddamn dictionary house going, 'Hey man, what am I supposed to say when I fuck my animal? You got no words for that. You guys gotta put a word there in the dictionary.'"

People were filing out. Entire rows were emptying. And while mothers and fathers pulled their kids down the aisle toward the exits by the arm and elderly golfers left in a huff, Macdonald moved on to how animals might feel about sex with humans. "I feel sorry for the animal, because it's not consenting," he said before reconsidering. "Maybe they're consenting, but we don't know. Maybe animals are going, 'Hey, I don't know why people are stopping this. I said Yes. No means No. I said fucking Oink. That's what I say when I want to get fucked—Oink.'"

"Also," he continued, "can you imagine if you're a pig and you're having sex with a beautiful lady and then afterward you gotta go home and fuck a pig? Before, you didn't know. You were like, 'Hey, this pig's all right.' You don't know it's a dirty pig. Then you're having sex with a beautiful lady. Then they're like, 'Hey, go fuck pigs again.' Like, 'You dirty bastard. You burned me.' What if you're watching one of those movies and you're saying, 'Hey, there's a pig fucking a lady?' And then you're like, 'Hey, wait a second. That's that lady who wouldn't dance with me last Friday.'"

It was, as the *Cedar Rapids Gazette* put it, "all too much."[19] Bowlsby told the papers that university officials were doing everything they could that night to get Macdonald off the stage. And according to Klatt, officials even contemplated *physically* pulling Macdonald off the stage. In the anniversary article, the night's host, Nate Soesbe, told the *Gazette*, "Whoever booked the show comes in the green room all sweaty with his tie askew. He looked like he had seen a ghost. He says, 'You gotta go get him.' 'Me, pull Norm off the stage? I'm not getting him.' Breuer was laughing. He says, 'I'm not getting him.'"

"I knew what Norm was doing," said Johnson. "I just knew his frustration level was high by the time he got onstage that he didn't care. Not that he wouldn't have done that material anyway. But I think he took great joy in watching people walk out."

In the end, it was estimated that 80 percent of the 1,300 people in attendance, which included "a number of children," had walked out during Macdonald's performance. So that's *a lot* of joy. "They weren't like, yelling. They weren't mean," Macdonald told Howard Stern shortly after the event.[20] "They just…quietly left."

Included in the 80 percent who left the theater was my mother, who took off in a hurry shortly after the pig joke started. And much to her dismay, Hancher Auditorium continued to pipe the sound of the show (and the rest of that pig joke) into the lobby, where she chose to wait for us for the remaining thirty-five minutes. The people who stayed, 260 or so, were loving every minute of it. "People were filing out in droves," one attendee remembered, "but there was a small group of college-aged kids there that were going crazy."

Of course, my friends and I were among those remaining 260 who were going crazy. To the point that I remember physically hurting from laughter. I'd never experienced anything like that before. And on the ride home, my very concerned mother told me the show would probably be in the papers the next day and that she should call the other boys' parents to warn them. "Your friends each told me that wasn't necessary because they had totally heard that kind of talk before," my mom remembered. One friend even tried to tell her that his family listened to things like that all the time. But until my mom told me the show would be in the papers, I'm not sure I knew that what I was seeing was historic or even newsworthy. And how could I? It was my first time seeing comedy in person. So I just knew it was incredibly special to *me*. And I definitely wasn't alone in that assessment.

"Me and Breuer knew something special was happening," Soesbe said. "He and I got chairs and sat on the side of the stage where nobody could see us. It was one of the most brilliant shows I've ever seen."

The next day, as my mom predicted, scathing reports of Macdonald's act started making the rounds in the papers. What followed was nothing short of a moral panic. At least regionally. "No laughing matter for Iowa" declared my hometown *Muscatine Journal* on June 24. "Iowa sports officials say they wish they hadn't invited comedian Norm Macdonald," the article began "and they don't plan to do it again." Macdonald had "references to sex acts, AIDS and homosexuality," said the *Cedar Rapids Gazette*. "From

Tuesday, June 24, 1997 | Sports | Muscatine Journal 3B

No laughing matter for Iowa

U of I athletic department regrets hiring "Saturday Night Live" comedian

IOWA CITY (AP) – Iowa sports officials say they wish they hadn't invited comedian Norm MacDonald and they don't plan to do it again.

MacDonald, who plays the anchor on the "Weekend Update" segment on "Saturday Night Live," was among the entertainers at a golf event that raises money for the athletic department.

His 50-minute routine at the university's Hancher Auditorium Sunday night was laced with profanity and sexual references, officials said, including jokes about women having sex with pigs.

"Norm MacDonald's performance was anything but comedy. It was profane, vulgar and off-color.
Iowa athletic director Bob Bowlsby

"Norm MacDonald's performance was anything but comedy," athletic director Bob Bowlsby said. "It was profane, vulgar and off-color. The last thing I want to do is suppress anybody's First Amendment rights, but I feel his material is inappropriate in the majority of venues in America."

Bowlsby, who issued the apology on behalf of the department, said about 80 percent of the people in the audience of 1,300, which included a number of children, walked out during MacDonald's performance.

Those who remained laughed and applauded the routine.

As people were leaving, MacDonald said, "What do you want me to talk about — losing my luggage at the airport?" He also said, "What do they expect — for me to hold up a picture of Yassir Arafat and make a joke?"

Rick Klatt, assistant athletic director for external affairs, said officials contemplated pulling MacDonald off stage, but he was allowed to finish his routine. His invitation to play in Monday's golf event was rescinded, said Bowlsby, who was among those who walked out.

The event was sponsored by AEGON, a worldwide financial management and insurance company with offices in Cedar Rapids and Baltimore. Bowlsby accepted full responsibility for scheduling MacDonald.

"Neither AEGON USA nor its many affiliated companies were involved in the screening or selection of program participants," Bowlsby said in a statement. "We regret the inclusion of Mr. MacDonald in an event sponsored by our department."

Two other "Saturday Night Live" actors, Darrell Hammond and Jim Breuer, also performed Sunday night, as did a local improvisation group, Comedy Sportz. Bowlsby called their performances "energetic and humorous."

Iowa student Brent Vanderschel said he felt MacDonald's humor was acceptable.

"Yeah, he was hilarious. He was just funny and deviant," Vanderschel told the Daily Iowan. "I think this is stuff people want to hear, at least the people that I went with wanted to hear this."

Many of the audience members who walked out were golfers in the tournament and athletic department staff.

"I think people didn't like him probably because they were older," Vanderschel said.

The aftermath of Norm Macdonald's Hancher performance. *From the* Muscatine Journal.

beginning to end, it was just one profanity after another," proclaimed the *Des Moines Register.* "His 50-minute routine…was laced with profanity and sexual references…including jokes about women having sex with pigs," said the *Journal.* Brian Duffy's political cartoon in the *Des Moines Register* on June 26 depicted Macdonald being yanked off stage by a long shepherd's hook. And, of course, I began collecting as many of the clippings as I could find, scanning my program onto our family's Macintosh Classic and sending it off to various Norm Macdonald fan sites whose early Internet webmasters were eager to get whatever information they could find. I was obviously a very cool kid.

In November 1997, *Rolling Stone* did a cover story about the cast of *Saturday Night Live.*[21] In the article, the reporter said that on the sparse walls of Macdonald's office were a portrait of Richard Nixon, a photo of Macdonald with Howard Stern and a bulletin board containing a snapshot of Macdonald's son, as well as two letters. One was from Bob Dole (whom Macdonald impersonated on the show), written in 1995, which said, "If you're ever in Washington and want to see the real article, please feel free to stop by my office. With two terms of a Dole presidency, I can keep you employed until the year 2004!" The other letter was from Rich Klatt, the University of Iowa's assistant athletic director for external affairs.

The letter was written on June 23, 1997, the day after the Hancher show. "This letter is to inform you," it began, "that the invitation to you and a guest to participate in the golf event on the University of Iowa campus later today has been formally withdrawn. Your performance last night at the Hancher Auditorium was inconsistent with values and morals of the staff of the University of Iowa Men's Athletic Department and the University of Iowa and Iowa City community as a whole. You insulted the intelligence and decency of a great many people with a monologue which was, at minimum, irresponsible."

When the *Rolling Stone* story hit the newsstands, it caused a new round of headlines in the local Iowa papers soon after. And Klatt told the *Gazette*,[22] "I'm glad I took the extra time to do it well, because it got published someplace." And then he added, "I can't image that if Bob Dole was sitting in Hancher Auditorium that night I was sitting there, that he'd be writing a letter telling [Macdonald] how funny he was."

Either way, Macdonald did not get the memo in time. "I [went] to the golf tournament," he told Stern and co-host Robin Quivers, "And this old guy goes, 'What are you doing here?' And I go, 'Remember, you invited me to the golf tournament?' And then the guy goes, 'You can't be in our golf tournament!' So then I was like, 'Oh, my God. I can't even be in the golf tournament? I came all this way.' And I didn't even want to go to the stupid golf tournament. So then I said, 'Oh, well, I might as well play golf.' So I went to the starters thing and then the guy [there] said, 'Okay, I'll shotgun you out to the 10th hole.' And the old guy heard it. He goes, 'I will not have him on the golf course!'"

Erin Doud-Johnson, Norm Macdonald and Jeff Johnson. *Jeff Johnson.*

In October 2008, Macdonald returned to Eastern Iowa to play Jeff Johnson's Penguins Comedy Club in Cedar Rapids. And Johnson made sure to bring up the Hancher show from 1997. "He thought it was really cool," Johnson told me. "He wasn't embarrassed by it at all. He thought it was funny and took pride in the fact that they wouldn't let him golf the next day."

Five years after Macdonald's Hancher set and about a mile away, I tried stand-up myself for the first time. But the Hancher show will forever be my origin story—and probably the reason I'm so interested in historically infamous sets in the first place. So I thought it also might be important to put the Norm story at the front of this book so you can enter into this world with me. As we've seen with Lenny Bruce, Richard Pryor and George Carlin (and then with Darrell Hammond and Jim Breuer), times, attitudes and morals can shift pretty significantly over time. The line will often move. So I'm not even sure what will offend you by the time you read this book and what will pass without a second thought. Yesterday's sex with a pig might be today's "tuchus." Or vice versa. I just know that, in 2025, a bestiality joke is still definitely not appropriate for an all-ages audience. But I also know that if you can't handle the late, great Norm Macdonald, you're probably not going to make it very far into this book. And that's fine. You can leave any time. But just know that, much like Hancher Auditorium in 1997, I'm just gonna keep piping the sound into the lobby.

Chapter 1

GOING DOWN IN F***ING FLAMES

Sometime in the late spring of 2024, I was at the Lyric Hyperion Theater in Los Angeles and approached veteran comedian and director Paul Provenza in the green room to ask him about a story. It's the story you're about to read. And it's the story that inspired this book. "I'm writing about the most infamous open mic set of all time," I told him. Except before the word *time* could even leave my mouth, he replied, "Is it about Kyle Parris?"

I smiled as we nodded knowingly. "Yes," I said, "it is." At least that's how I remember it.

Known as the "Paris of the Plains," the "Barbecue Capital of the World" and the "Heart of America," Kansas City has been home to such cultural icons as Charlie Parker, Walt Disney, Ernest Hemingway and Satchel Paige. It's a cradle of jazz, the birthplace of the Happy Meal and the center of the pop culture universe any time Tay is in town to watch Trav play.

And in July 2001, Kansas City was also the setting where a twentysomething aspiring comedian named Kyle Parris went onstage at Stanford & Sons in the entertainment district of Westport and performed what can only be described as the most infamous open mic set in the history of stand-up comedy.

This is no easy task. Open mics are simultaneously the most essential aspect of every comedian's development and a free-for-all open forum for drifters, scoundrels and lunatics. If you're lucky, an open mic will show you the future of comedy. If you're unlucky, which is a whole lot more likely, you will never find a more wretched hive of scum and villainy. And probably body odor. Ask any veteran comedian and they'll tell you about some goddamned deranged thing they've seen at an open mic or heard about from an open mic, and each story is more disturbing than the last. But of all the horrific stories I've heard about all the terrible open mic sets in all the gin joints in all the towns in all the world, one set takes the cake as the most horrific and terriblest of them all.

But this didn't just happen in any old club. No, no. That would be too easy. The most infamous open mic set in the history of stand-up also happens to have taken place in one of the most infamous clubs in the modern history of stand-up—owned and operated by one of the most notorious and colorful families in modern stand-up since the decades following Prohibition, when show business was run by families with names like Genovese, Gambino and the Chicago Outfit. Just to give you an idea what we're talking about, a former GM of Stanford & Sons told me that 85 to 90 percent of anything I hear about the club is probably true. And the worse it is, the more likely.

I'd heard the story of this open mic set for years with many wild variations. My personal favorite is told enthusiastically by comedian Brendan McGowan. But to quote Bob Dole, I wanted the "real article." So I tracked down as many of the eyewitnesses, contemporary accounts and veterans of the Kansas City comedy scene as I could find to help me piece together this epic saga—including the man whose set started me on my journey down the dark and labyrinthine Stanford & Sons rabbit hole in the first place. This story is true, to the best of all their collective memories. It is also one of the most unreal things I've ever heard in my life.

The story of this particular set probably begins around 2000, when Parris, like many young men at the time, was a huge fan of comedian and MTV star Tom Green. Except, unlike most of those young men, Parris actually wanted to *be* Tom Green—or at least to emulate his wild and shocking comedic ways. So when Parris picked up a copy of *Rolling Stone* magazine and read that Green once pulled a dead raccoon out of a suitcase on a Canadian talk show,[23] his imagination went into overdrive. "I was like, 'That's fucking nuts,'" Parris said.[24] "I would never do that. But if I *did*...what would it be like?'"

So, Parris wrote out a sketch—with no real intention of ever actually doing it—where he played an animal trainer whose animals jumped through hoops and did a variety of other tricks. Except instead of bringing a *live* animal to the performance, Parris would find roadkill on the way to the show, and then, once he'd revealed his prized animal, he would feign shock and horror when he discovered it had "died." Then Parris, as animal

Kyle Parris in a recent image. *Kyle Parris.*

trainer, would say something like, "Oh, my gosh! I think my animal is choking!" And then he would produce a vacuum cleaner from behind a curtain and use its nozzle to suck whatever was "choking" this thing out of its throat. And when that attempt inevitably failed, he'd shout, "Oh, my God! My animal's dead! What are we gonna do?" And then he'd decide the show must go on.

At this point, the plan—in what I should remind you was an innocent, hypothetical, never-to-actually-be-done sketch—was to take the dead animal and throw its body through a hoop, hard enough to smack against the back wall. Then he'd announce that his animal was going to do some backflips. And he would launch the animal into the air until it slammed up against the ceiling and then splatted back down to the stage. And finally, he'd pick the roadkill back up, grab its paw and make it wave goodbye to the crowd. And that was gonna be the act.

"It sounded great on paper," he said. And sure. Why not? It was just a writing exercise, after all. "I was like, 'Yeah, this would be so funny if I actually did it,'" Parris said. "But I'm not gonna do it."

By this point, if you couldn't tell from his zany roadkill sketch, in the early 2000s, Parris was definitely known around the Kansas City comedy scene for having a pretty unusual act. And I'll tell you more specifics later. But he was probably just as well known for his unusual appearance as for what he did onstage. The *Kansas City Star* once said that Parris was most notable for having a "mass of frizzy, brown hair hovering several inches above his scalp."[25] Comedian Chris Porter described Parris's look as "Kramer [from *Seinfeld*] on acid…Michael Richards if you were fucking four hours deep." And Parris described himself to me as having a "big ass Afro," a "long face" and a "hooked nose." He was a unique-looking guy, is what I'm telling you. And I only mention his looks because I feel like it doesn't hurt this already weird story.

Parris got his start in stand-up in Kansas City back in 1998 and immediately grew tired of the standard setup/punchline format. "I decided to put aside regular jokes," he told me, "and focus on doing one-person sketches." And probably partly because of the release of the Andy Kaufman biopic *Man on the Moon* in late 1999, the comparison between Parris and Kaufman became inevitable wherever he went. But while he admits to liking a few of Kaufman's classic bits, Parris was more into classic *Saturday Night Live* sketches, particularly Dan Aykroyd's "Bass-O-Matic" routine from 1976. "When you see the fish being put into the actual blender," he said, "that was the funniest fucking thing I'd ever seen."

Which brings us back to Tom Green and the dead raccoon. On a summer night in 2001, a year after Parris wrote his own dead animal sketch and filed it away forever, he went to an open mic and became demoralized by the reaction to another set he did. Or, I suppose, the lack of reaction. "I got zero laughs," he told me. "I failed so fucking hard. Then the other comics were doing just regular, run-of-the-mill, garden variety jokes and were doing well. And I was so pissed by that. Like, 'Goddammit, I'm trying to do something *different*. And trying to offer something that's unusual, that you don't see with any other comic'…I left the show that night thinking, 'You know what? If I'm gonna go down, I'm gonna go down in fucking flames.'"

So, Kyle Parris decided right then and there that he was actually going to do the roadkill sketch he'd written the year before. And he was going to do it at the open mic the following Monday on the very stage where he'd just failed so miserably.

Chapter 2
STANFORD'S

As far as settings for weird comedy stories go, it would be hard to pick a more appropriate location than Stanford & Sons (aka "Stanford's") in Westport. It's essentially its own character in the story and worthy of a proper introduction. We'll return to the Kyle Parris story in a bit. But if we use a Kansas City jazz analogy, just think of him as the head arrangement in a Count Basie or Charlie Parker song and know that some of these players are so good that we've got to give them extended solos.

The original Stanford & Sons building itself was at 504 Westport Road—in the Chouteau-Bridger Building, once owned by famed mountain man Jim Bridger.[26] Historically, Westport was also one of the main starting points for the Oregon Trail, as well as a pit stop on the Santa Fe Trail. And the building directly next to the old Stanford's building—now Kelly's Westport Inn—was an outfitter for wagon trains heading west. Both the Chouteau-Bridger Building and Kelly's (aka the Albert G. Boone Store) were built in 1851 and 1850, respectively, which would make them the two oldest buildings in Kansas City.

It also means that both buildings survived the Battle of Westport in 1864, also known as the "Gettysburg of the West." Participants in the Civil War battle included Buffalo Bill Cody and Wild Bill Hickok. All of this serves as a helpful reminder that this place was and is straight out of the Wild West. And just like in the days of Buffalo Bill, Wild Bill or Bridger himself, Stanford's boasted a colorful cast of crooked lawmen, outlaws and swindlers. And yes, I'm being literal.

"That family were true outlaws," veteran comedian Mike Saccone told me about the club's owners. "In every sense of the word. I mean, they were criminals. And they were drug dealers. They were bank embezzlers, drug addicts....But I got along with all of them, as crazy as they were. I loved the whole 'Jack Kerouac scene' of it. You know? The comedy club's run by a bunch of crazy drug addicts? Cool. *Perfect.*"

Stanford's had a family patriarch, Stan Glazer, who reads like a flamboyant combination of Fred Trump, Ric Flair and a made-for-TV-movie car salesman played by Dennis Farina. "He was crazy," Saccone confirmed. "He was a wild man. He was, like, this old-school rich guy that needed people to know that he was the boss and he ran the joint. He was this big voice. And he kind of looked like an old school movie star too. He was a good-looking guy with a barrel chest and a manicured mustache. And he'd go into the restaurant in the middle of rush hour—it was a very popular restaurant, good food—and he would get in an argument on the phone loudly hollering at his Porsche dealer that his race car better be finished by Friday or heads will roll. He was like a cartoon rich guy."

"He was a playboy right out of Central Casting," Craig Glazer, Stan's eldest son, said of his father, in a slightly more complimentary description. "A cross between Dean Martin and Cesar Romero. He was tall, handsome, funny, creative, a big time storyteller, and the offspring of a family of hustlers."

Opposite: Stanford & Sons, circa 1980. *Missouri Valley Special Collections.*

Above: The corner of Westport and Pennsylvania, 1892. *Missouri Valley Special Collections.*

Right: Jim Bridger Monument. *Missouri Valley Special Collections.*

"My dad, married or not, was a ladies' man," Craig continued. "Many of his business acquaintances figured he had already screwed their wives or that it was only a matter of time before he did."[27]

Stan Glazer. *Greg Edwards.*

"Hey, I was just a Dean Martin–looking guy," Stan told the *Kansas City Star* in response to that very accusation. "[T]hat's just the way things were back then. I make no apologies about that….I was the one who was approached for the affairs, I never solicited them."[28]

"Mind you, Stan Glazer [was] eighty years old," comedian David Naster added. "And he's in Bally's gyms working out and he got kicked out for hitting on women. That's Stan Glazer. I mean, to know him is to love him. And to know him is to hate him." As former Stanford's president Larry Marks put it, "Nobody's on the fence about Stan."

Stanford & Sons—the restaurant and not yet the comedy club—opened its doors in 1975 to rave reviews and world-renowned patrons. Notable figures like Muhammad Ali, Clint Eastwood, Gerald Ford and Ronald Reagan, plus baseball gods like George Brett and Roger Clemens, all reportedly dropped in over the years and enjoyed specialties like the flower pot bread.[29] But before he had this one successful venture, or any flower pot bread to speak of, Stan Glazer was mostly known around Kansas City for failing in several other businesses while continuing to live large, buy big houses and drive fancy cars.[30] "If he made $5,000," his ex-wife told the *Kansas City Star* in 2000, "he would spend $10,000."

"From what I understand," comedian Tim Gaither told me, "[the Glazer kids] grew up in a house that didn't have a stick of furniture in it because [Stan] wanted to keep up appearances."

The restaurant, whose name was certainly capitalizing on the popularity of the 1970s NBC sitcom *Sanford and Son*, was also an opportunity for Stan to mend his broken relationship with his sons, Craig, Jeff and Jack, to whom he hadn't been much of a father. The boys still idolized their bad boy old man, whose own example had led them to believe that it was okay to bend the rules. After all, they did get into Chiefs football games for free when Stan would flash an honorary deputy sheriff's badge at security and claim that the boys were visiting from an orphanage. "I learned from Stan that you could get away with anything," Craig said, "if you were clever enough."[31]

Craig and his brothers, it would be fair to say, were not always clever enough. And they often wound up behind bars because of it. As comedian Steve Kramer put it in an animated short about Stanford & Sons, "If the Jesse James brothers made love to the Three Stooges, their children would be the Glazer brothers."[32]

Middle brother Jeff would often get arrested for theft, a crime he was allegedly committing to pay for his increasingly expensive heroin addiction. He and youngest brother Jack would sometimes set up scams where one of them would go into a bank and lure away the teller while the other would lean over the counter and steal cash from their register. And a number of comics have heard one wacky anecdote or another involving some harebrained reason why Jeff and/or Jack had been arrested. "One time when they robbed the bank they were so high that they forgot to wear a disguise," Kramer told me.

"One of them robbed a liquor store and the getaway car had the personalized tags 'GLAZER 1,'" comedian Justin Leon said. And still, Jeff and Jack's outlaw lifestyle paled in comparison to the one led by eldest brother Craig.

As chronicled in his memoir, *The King of Sting*, Craig began selling weed as a student at Arizona State and was robbed at gunpoint by another drug dealer. That's when he went vigilante, setting up a series of *thirty-three* fake sting operations in order to get revenge on that dealer and, I suppose, the drug world at large. Craig set out for Hollywood in 1981 with his partner in crime, Don Woodbeck, to pitch his own true "drug dealer Robin Hood" story to movie execs.

The execs were biting too, at least for a while. The president of CBS Theatrical called Craig and Woodbeck "a modern day Butch and Sundance" in the *L.A. Times* in 1981. While they were out in Hollywood, the two bandits rubbed elbows with movie stars. And things actually got far enough along in the development process that NBC sent *Today* show cameramen to Stanford & Sons to secretly record the sting artists buying heroin from a dealer in order to bust up a local ring.[33]

The publicity was supposed to enhance their chances of getting the movie greenlit and launch Craig and Woodbeck into stardom. Hell, they were even taking acting classes to play themselves in the movie.[34] But all that press was drawing unwanted attention to heroin usage in Kansas City and caused blowback from local authorities. And in the end, it just kinda seemed like the whole thing was faked for cameras anyway. Probably because it had been faked for cameras—a detail Craig wouldn't fully cop to until the release of his book twenty-seven years later.

The *Today* show producers were the first industry gatekeepers to get cold feet. Then CBS Theatrical eventually dropped the project as well. And then, in a Hollywood twist that caused me to blurt out "holy shit" as I followed along in the newspaper headlines more than four decades later, Woodbeck was eventually found shot to death "in the bathtub of a fashionable Redondo Beach apartment" in 1982.[35]

I'll dive into the details more fully in a later chapter, but when questions arose over the duo's credibility, Woodbeck had apparently attempted to pull off one more sting to prove his bona fides.[36] Or maybe he'd become addicted to the adrenaline rush provided by the stings. Either way, it cost him his life. Craig had been standing by a nearby elevator at the time of the murder and left the scene as soon as he heard gunshots. He called his agent, but not the police.

The story somehow gets even more complicated from there. Because shortly after he went straight (in between his time as the "King of Sting" and having an agent in Hollywood), Craig was an agent himself—the special kind. As in, Craig Glazer transitioned from being a metaphorical drug world Robin Hood to working as a crooked cop for the metaphorical Sheriff of Nottingham. "Glazer was one of our best agents," Kansas's controversial former attorney general Vern Miller told the *Kansas City Times*[37] in 1974.

Vern fucking Miller. Now *this* is a character. The press called him the "Super Sheriff," an apt nickname indeed. In February 1971, six weeks after taking office, Miller made good on his campaign promise to "leap into the drug-ridden hippie communities of Lawrence with both feet" by leading 150 officers into the University of Kansas campus in the biggest raid in state history.[38] According to the *Wichita Eagle*, 33 suspected drug offenders were arrested and a "large amount of marijuana and LSD was confiscated in the raids."[39]

It was good enough to get Miller voted as top newsmaker in all of Kansas for 1971 by newspaper and broadcast editors polled by United Press International. "That was only the beginning," said the *Eagle*. "Through the year Miller has led or planned major drug raids in virtually all corners of the state, including simultaneous raids on the 15 cities from Lawrence to Garden City [on] July 21 that netted 50 suspects and involved 200 officers."

"He personally led some of those raids," said the *Eagle*.[40] "On one occasion, Miller popped out of a car trunk like a jack-in-the-box to make an arrest and on another, he climbed out onto a housetop in hot pursuit of a suspect."

In *The King of Sting*, Craig said that Miller once "nabbed a suspected dealer, put on his clothes, and went to a party where the suspect had been expected in order to gain information."

"He's one of the few people that all the crazy stories you read about him are true—and in fact are typically not the craziest stories that are actually out there," said Sedgwick County District Attorney Marc Bennett of Miller in 2021.[41]

In 1972, Miller cracked down on the sale of liquor aboard Amtrak trains crossing through the state at a time when public drinking in Kansas was against the law. "The comparison to the old-time, ax-swinging days of Carry Nation in Kansas is inevitable," said the *Kansas City Star*, referring to the famous radical anti-alcohol activist from pre-Prohibition days, notorious for raiding saloons and smashing their liquor bottles with her hatchet.[42] "Of course Miller could have gone to court, seeking a restraining order or injunction against the government corporation which now operates the passenger trains, for alleged violation of Kansas laws against public by-the-drink liquor sales. But the quiet route has not been his style."

No, it was not. And so Vern Miller inevitably became national news. By the following year, Johnny Carson was poking fun at him in his monologues. The guy was seemingly everywhere. "Club cars have been raided, railroad bartenders arrested and gallons of liquor confiscated as Amtrak passenger trains pass through the state," said the *Los Angeles Times* of Miller in 1973.[43] "Airlines have been ordered by the state of Kansas to stop serving drinks while flying over its territorial skies. Elderly women have been arrested for playing bingo. Slot machines have been smashed. Racetracks have been closed. And the man responsible, Vern Miller, 44, was reelected last November by one of the largest majorities in the state's history—70 percent of the vote."

How did the King of Sting get a job with the Super Sheriff in the first place? "My uncle Mort owned the Glazer Chemical Company," Craig explained. "Besides flying around the Midwest for business and performing as a stunt pilot at air shows, he'd take his friends up for fun. He would occasionally fly with Vern Miller."

And supposedly, when Miller came across Craig's FBI dossier, he decided to offer him a job. "You've got to have people working as agents who know the drug trade," the raid-happy Miller explained. "We're not dealing with a bunch of Sunday school boys or Boy Scouts."

In a very non–Boy Scout move, Craig wound up planting cocaine on innocent people in an attempt to drum up more publicity for Miller and boost his gubernatorial chances in the 1974 election. And it severely backfired—to the extent that Miller lost the election (by only 0.49 percent of the vote), and the *Kansas City Star* referred to Craig as "the kid who shot down Vern Miller."[44]

Vern Miller, who had been accused of political grandstanding as early as 1971, wasn't the type to forget who shot him down. And when Craig and Woodbeck's vigilante story began to be questioned openly in the national press in 1982, Miller told the *Los Angeles Times*, "I wouldn't believe what those guys told me if there was only three of us left in the world." And by 1983, he told the *Kansas City Times*, "I have nothing to say about those bastards."

In his memoir, Craig said that Miller "had all of the charisma and savvy needed in politics. If he had become governor, who knows where he might have gone from there…the governor's office might have led him to become President of the United States. I might have cost America a lot of entertainment."

Craig would cost America even more entertainment eleven years later. His movie pitch went into development hell after 1985, when he was sentenced to seven years in federal prison for conspiring to sell ten pounds of cocaine to undercover agents.[45] And he might have gotten even more time if not for a character-testimonial letter written by actual future Republican nominee for president (and seemingly prolific letter writer) Bob Dole. Ever the publicity hound himself, Craig's defense was that he'd "set out to 'sting' high-level drug dealers in the Los Angeles area on whom he blamed his partner's death."[46]

We'll stick a pin in Craig's Hollywood dreams for now. But along the way, the Glazer family would make at least one pretty solid show business decision. But as you're about to see, it would take some convincing to do so.

Chapter 3

BOOM

In early 1980, a comedian and street performer named David Naster approached Stan Glazer and his restaurant manager, Ron Maude, about using the upstairs "Tree House" room at Stanford & Sons for a comedy show.[47] The pitch did not go well. "Stan Glazer said, 'No goddamned comic is gonna come in here and do a goddamned comedy show and piss off my [customers],'" Naster remembered.

At that point, Kansas City had no comedy scene to speak of. There had really only been one guy—a tuxedo-clad guitar act named Calvin Coolidge (a fifth cousin of the thirtieth president) who had been knocking around town for about a decade.[48] "He performed at the Playboy Club," Naster said, "and just kinda told old jokes. Then he sang little parody songs."

"Calvin Coolidge was the biggest name in front of Naster in Kansas City," comedian Emery Emery said. "He's a guy who had one foot in kind of vaudevillian style performance, and another foot in the new comedy."

Coolidge was well paid for that act. He drove around town in a silver 1953 Bentley. And he may have had a leg up on the young upstart comedians in Kansas City, but David Naster had just spent a few months out in Los Angeles, where he'd been offered a spot as an unpaid regular at the Comedy Store by the club's famous owner, Mitzi Shore. It certainly wasn't *nothing*. And Naster knew that he needed to use whatever Hollywood cachet he had back at Stanford's if he was gonna sway the boss.

"I said, 'Stan, I don't know if you know this,'" Naster told me. "'[Mitzi Shore] rejects far more than she accepts....Let's do [a show] on Sunday nights, because that's an off night for you. We'll bring comics in. We'll advertise it. And then we'll just see how it goes.' And the bottom line, Mike—it caught on."

That is an understatement. From just Sundays, Naster's "Comedy House" expanded to Wednesdays, then Thursdays, then Fridays and then Saturdays. This eventually made Stanford & Sons the area's first comedy club. "We were kinda like, the cool guys in Westport for a short little bit," comedian Mike Saccone told me. "We were the new shiny thing. Girls hung around. Suddenly we were all getting laid and carrying on like, 'Oh, showbiz is working out.'"

David Naster. *Greg Edwards.*

Stan didn't necessarily love sharing attention with the new comics. "We got on the cover of the *Star* magazine," Saccone said, "because people were interested in the comedy thing….The photographer comes down and they picked a couple comedians to be on the cover—myself and a couple other guys. And we're all fucking excited…. And Stan shows up and railroads the whole thing, and he pushes us all aside and he goes, 'These comedians are not on the cover. This is gonna be about me. I'm Stan Glazer. I own the place.' And he's got a rattan chair all set up where he's gonna put a waitress on either knee…and he's gonna put his arms around them. And it's gonna be him on the cover. And the photographer goes, 'Look, this story is not about you or your restaurant. This story is about the comedians and the comedy club. And if you want this article, you need to move over. We're putting the comedians on the cover.'"

According to Saccone, Stan lost it. "He starts yelling at the photographer," he continued. "[He said,] 'Fuck the *Kansas City Star*! I've been around here for years without your fucking help! I don't need you pricks around here! Get the fuck out of here!' So he blows it. He ruins the whole thing for us. So we're thinking, '*Great.* We're not gonna be on the cover.' So the [photographer] kind of taps us and goes, 'Meet me outside in the parking lot.' So we meet the photographer in the parking lot. And he goes, 'Look, I know that you guys want this, and you should have it. So we'll reschedule the shoot at the *Star*'…And he did. So they did the article and put us on the cover. But [Stan] nearly screwed himself out of an article."

David Naster. *David Naster.*

One night at Stanford's in 1982 is still especially memorable for Saccone. "It was a Saturday night," he told me. "The place was pretty popular by now. So it was packed.…And I was standing in the lobby. I was the emcee. And there was a guy from Denver on, Ed Nichols. He was the headliner at the time. I'd just brought him up.…And in walks this guy [who] stands right next to me. He had a little beret on and sunglasses. And I was standing real close to him. We just caught eyes and I realized, holy shit, this is Robin Williams—when Robin Williams was just hot as a pistol [and] still doing stand-up [in] big arenas. And he kinda nods and walks past me and sits down. And I start freaking out, telling everybody, 'Robin Williams is here! *Robin Williams* is here!'"

Williams was in town to do a show the following night at the Starlight Theatre, where he'd play to 3,655 howling fans, as the *Kansas City Star* put it.[49] And Saccone decided to ask Williams if he'd like to go on. "To which the management said, 'Well, if he goes on, he can't run long because we have a second show,'" Saccone told me. "I said, 'Look, guys. This is *Robin Williams.* You are so lucky if he goes on [or] even touches the stage in this place. He's gonna do whatever he wants to do.'"

After management relented, Saccone says he approached Williams, who actually seemed eager to perform. "So I go to the back of the room," Saccone told me, "and I catch the gaze of the guy onstage, and I'm giving him the 'cut throat' sign [like,] 'Get off, get off, *get the fuck off.*' And he'd only been on for about ten minutes. And he's looking at me like, 'What's wrong?' Like, he's being fired or something….So he gets off, and I go up and I said, 'Folks, the show's not over. Don't worry. We have a special guest that's shown up. Please welcome Robin Williams.' And there's this silence and kind of a laugh, like, '*Ha ha.* What's the joke?' Up walks Robin Williams. And the place goes *berserk.* Like Elvis just walked in the room—this little ninety-seat room in Kansas City. Like, 'What the *fuck*?!?' And he proceeds to just murder the place for forty-five minutes. Jumping all over. Running into the crowd. Grabbing people. Such an intimate scene. And he's just this dynamo—famous, cocaine-fueled Robin Williams. And [he] just kills and then drifts off into the night."

Stanford & Sons, Inc.
An Eating & Drinking Establishment
Operating Account
504 Westport Road
Kansas City, Mo 64111

1882

83-1038
1010

Feb 27 1981

Pay to the order of Elliot Threat $50.00/xx

Stanford & Sons, Inc. 50 DOLS 00 CTS Dollars

The Shawnee State Bank
11101 Johnson Drive Shawnee, Kansas 66203

President

Elliott Threatt's first comedy paycheck. *Elliott Threatt.*

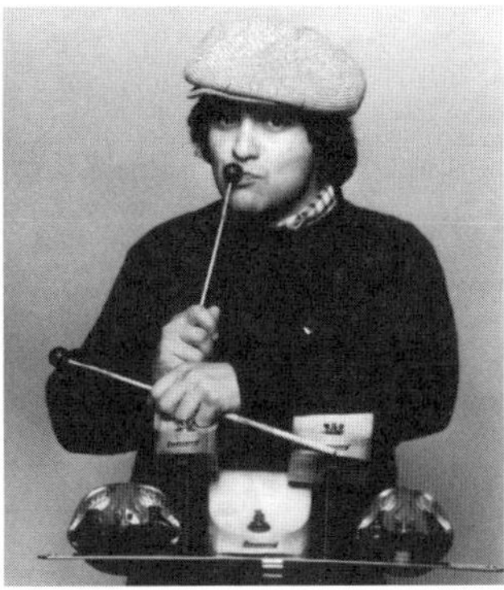

Left: Louie Anderson (*left*), David Naster (*center front*) and Henny Youngman (*center*), 1981 Midwest Comedy Competition. *David Naster*.

Right: David Naster. *David Naster*.

Before long, everybody in the area knew that Robin Williams had come by Stanford & Sons. "When Robin Williams came in, that was like jet fuel to everything," veteran Kansas City comic Elliott Threatt said.

While the club got more and more popular in Westport, David Naster continued to tour the country and make connections in the booming world of '80s stand-up, which was inventing itself as it went along. "For like, the first year it was just us—this handful of [Kansas City] guys," Saccone said. "And then Naster went up to Minneapolis and played. And he made connections with all those guys—Louie Anderson…Joel Madison, Joel Hodgson, Jeff Cesario, Alex Cole, Emo Philips from Chicago…Judy Tenuta….And so they started coming to town as headliners for three or four days a week…they were a little older than us, a little farther along in the process."

"We had this kind of weird camaraderie," Threatt said, "between the [Kansas City] comics and Denver [comics], who came over all the time, the comics in Minneapolis who came all the time. And St. Louis. Those were, like, our sister cities."

"There were not many clubs open [in the country]," former Stanford's president Larry Marks said of that early '80s period. "[There were] a couple of East Coast clubs. I think we were well before most of the Denver stuff and the Texas stuff. And they used us as a stopover while they were traveling. Some nights, I'd end up with five headliner comics [who] all showed up on a Sunday to take a layover because we had a show. And we'd just put them up like a big round robin of comics."

One particular night at Stanford's, "This real tall Black guy comes in," Naster said. "And he's six-four, and he looks down at me and goes, 'Yo, Mr. Naster. I'm thinking about doing some comedy, man….I just drove up from Wichita, man.' I said, 'Yeah, I'll put you on. Wanna go on tonight? What's your name?' He goes, 'Uh, Sinbad. They call me Sinbad.'"

That night, according to everyone who witnessed it, Sinbad (government name: David Adkins) absolutely knocked it out of the park. In the parlance of comedy, he killed. He crushed. He destroyed. "The place went crazy," Naster said. "Then Louie Anderson goes up after him and says, 'Man, I wish I could talk that way.' And he starts imitating the way Sinbad talks…. And the audience fucking started booing him. *Hated* him. Because they loved Sinbad."

"I saw David Naster work that night and I said to myself, 'That's what I want to do,'" Sinbad told the *Kansas City Star* in 1991.[50] "[From] the moment I started, I loved it."

"[Sinbad] was just absolutely, like, out-of-the-box dynamically funny and animated," Saccone said. "And he would go up every night with a brand new set—something he read that day in a magazine. He would go up and he would just murder. For like, ten minutes. [He came] out of nowhere. It was just astonishing, the stage presence."

"Anybody that went on after Sinbad had a bit of a struggle," Naster said. "Because he worked the audience. And he was so likable."

He must have been. Because in hindsight, it is pretty astonishing just how fast Sinbad went from abject poverty to stardom. "I lived out of my car for like a year and a half," he told the *Kansas City Star* in 1986.[51] "I would pull up and sleep behind the Holiday Inn….I'd get up in the morning and I'd try to find a room that the maids were cleaning. I'd run in and take a shower."

Sinbad. *Greg Edwards.*

Sinbad had been stationed at McConnell Air Force Base in Wichita but was told to leave for, as he told it, "acting crazy on the base" in 1982. "I would impersonate officers. I went AWOL. I was belligerent. I got an honorable under general conditions [discharge]. That means, 'You're a bad boy and we want to try to mess your life up as much as we can when you get out.'"

But if you believe his story, Sinbad had just won an air force talent show, and his bad behavior was a ploy to get out of his service and pursue comedy. There is another version among some people where he went AWOL out of embarrassment that he didn't make the air force basketball team. But either way, it all worked out. Sinbad would catch the bus to Kansas City on weekends and perform his first gigs at Stanford & Sons. And like everyone else in the scene, David Naster was blown away by Sinbad's talent. So Naster convinced him to move from Wichita to Kansas City and offered him the love seat in his living room as a place to crash.

"So Sinbad's staying with me," Naster said. "I said, 'Sinbad, I gotta tell you, man. One day you're gonna be huge. You're just gonna be huge.' And he goes, 'Oh, come on, man.' I said, 'No, Sinbad. I've seen comics. It's what I do for a living. I've never seen anybody do what you do."

"[Sinbad] could read names out of a phone book," Threatt said. "He was there very quickly and out very quickly. I mean, he came in and took everything over like a whirlwind....And then, next thing you know, he was on [the popular '80s television competition show] *Star Search*."

Once Sinbad landed on television in the mid-'80s, his career was off to the races. He won on *Star Search* seven times (including a victory over Dennis Miller) in 1985 before losing in the finals to John Kassir, who would later voice the Cryptkeeper on HBO's *Tales from the Crypt*. From there, Sinbad became the warm-up comic on *The Cosby Show* before landing his most famous role as Coach Walter Oakes on the *Cosby Show* spinoff series *A Different World* from 1987 to 1991.

It seems Naster had quite an eye for talent in those days. One night at the Comedy Works in Denver, that eye spotted a talented young female comic whom he decided to take on tour. Her name was Roseanne Barr. "I'm the first comic to ever take Roseanne on the road," Naster said. And eventually that road would lead both back to Kansas City.

One night at Stanford's, at least according to Naster, he hosted a show that would include pre-fame Roseanne, pre-fame Sinbad and Minneapolis comic (and future *Roseanne* sitcom writer) Joel Madison, who happened to bring a friend. "Joel calls me the day before coming," Naster said. "He goes, 'I got a friend from Ottumwa, Iowa, that I want to bring.' So I walk in with Sinbad and Roseanne. Standing there in the lobby, right before we go into the Tree House, is Joel Madison and Tom Arnold. And that's where [Tom and Roseanne] met for the first time."

Arnold and Barr, of course, wound up in a tumultuous marriage from 1990 to 1994, which became constant fodder for tabloids, as well as for two separate made-for-TV movies (*Roseanne & Tom: Behind the Scenes* and *Roseanne: An Unauthorized Biography*) in 1994. And because of Arnold's settlement (he took home a reported $50 million from Roseanne), it also became one of the most infamous divorces of all time.

Stanford & Sons kinda seems like the perfect place for that couple to have met. And it is technically possible. But alas, Arnold disputes this story, although he did concede that he and Roseanne worked Stanford & Sons together on multiple occasions. But Arnold believes that he and Roseanne met at the Minneapolis Comedy Gallery in 1983, adding, "I can't believe anyone wants credit for introducing Roseanne and I."

That being said, Naster definitely deserves credit for *something*. Years later, Stanford & Sons—particularly Craig Glazer—publicly took credit for Sinbad's success and boasted about his involvement in early appearances by Roseanne Barr, Louie Anderson and Robin Williams.[52] "Craig Glazer wasn't anywhere around," Naster said of that period. "Once Stanford's started going a little bit, Jeff and Craig started coming around a little more. And they start working the door. Because they're taking cash. That's all I'll say about that."

Naster stepped away from Stanford's in 1983. "Being around Craig and Stan for a period of time can wear on a man's soul," he told me. Naster did make an appearance on *Star Search* the following year, losing what he's pretty sure was a rigged-for-TV matchup against Rosie O'Donnell in the process. It was the same year *Star Search* launched the career of Sinbad.[53] Still, Naster looks back on this period fondly, even though he should probably be

Left: David Naster. *David Naster.*

Right: David Naster, NACA College Comedian of the Year. *David Naster.*

celebrated a bit more as the godfather and originator of the Kansas City comedy scene.

"Here's the deal," he told me. "I know I [started the scene]. Other comics who were there during that time know I did it. And that's really all that matters."

Not only do the comics from that period know it was Naster who started the scene, but many also still consider him one of the greatest comedians they've ever seen, period. "David had the chops to be a big national star," Craig wrote in 2011, "he just didn't get lucky like Sinbad who was not his equal."[54]

Sinbad himself hasn't forgotten his first champion. "One day he called me," Naster said. "He goes, 'Yo, Naster. Hey, man. I gotta thank you. Man, I remember the time I didn't have any money and you sent me some money. I remember those times you bought me some clothes, man. I'll never forget that, man. You took care of me when I needed it. Thank you, man.' I said, 'You're welcome.' *He hangs up*."

Throughout the '80s, several other stars came through Stanford's—at multiple locations—including Jerry Seinfeld, Sam Kinison and Bill Hicks. "If you went through the list of comics that appeared on HBO specials and [*The*] *Tonight Show*," Marks said, "we probably worked with 50 percent of them."[55]

The club is also where a young Eddie Griffin got his start. And although his stint there seems to have been short, it has generated a lot of lore. According to Griffin himself, he and his cousin were out at a show at Stanford's one night in 1989 and weren't exactly impressed with what they saw.[56] "My cousin is like, 'Man, you funnier than these folks. You should go on up there,'" Griffin said. Then his cousin "waved a $50 bill in [Griffin's] face for incentive. The club owner agreed to give Griffin three minutes onstage; Griffin took 45. And killed."

Nevertheless, "[Griffin] never caught on with Stanford's," the *Kansas City Star* said in 1992, "because, in the words of president Larry Marks, his material never developed and he had to be asked to tone down his profanity and shock-value humor. Griffin says he was simply a black comedian unable to fit a white comedy club's idea of funny."[57]

"One of my more infamous stories," Marks chucked when I asked him in 2024 for the uncensored version. "You might have to [bleep] a lot of this conversation, but [Griffin] would come on open mic night just full of piss and vinegar—all the energy in the world. And he'd go up onstage and, to be honest with you, almost every routine he did had a slathering of 'pussy, motherfucker, n----' in it."

The last straw seems to be when Griffin convinced Marks to let him open for a headliner who worked clean. "He burnt me really bad," Marks remembered. "He said, 'No, I got this show on MTV....I gotta do three clean minutes, so I'll practice it.' So he got up onstage and did 'pussy, n----, motherfucker,' and I actually was coming to the stage to throw him off—went and turned off the lights....And he was onstage [saying,] 'See, that's how they treat us around this club and blah blah blah'...And I said, 'Eddie, that's it. I gave you every chance in the world.'"

With precious few other places in Kansas City to perform, Griffin set off for Los Angeles shortly after. "He was in and out of Kansas City like *that*," Emery told me, snapping his fingers for effect. "He was too big for Kansas City the first time he stepped onstage there. And he behaved that way. And then decided he's gonna come out to Hollywood."

Eddie Griffin. *Greg Edwards.*

"And it's like, '*Good luck with that*,'" Elliott Threatt said of his decision to move. "And then, like, six months later, it's like, 'Did you hear Eddie Griffin's opening up for Andrew Dice Clay?' Because Andrew Dice Clay was huge at the time. It's like, 'Oh, my God. How did that happen so quickly?' It was like, a nanosecond. But he kind of always resented Stanford's and never came back."

The club loved to take credit for Griffin nonetheless. An extra wrinkle to the Griffin-Stanford's story is that Griffin's UPN sitcom *Malcolm & Eddie* took place at Kelly's Westport Inn, the rival bar at 500 Westport Road—directly next to Stanford & Sons. And most veterans of the scene have told me they saw that as a not-so-subtle dig at the Glazers. "It was basically the Hatfields and the McCoys between Stanford's and Kelly's," former Stanford's GM Ron Meurrens told me. "Eddie Griffin did that to [tell] Craig and Stan to go fuck themselves."

"Eddie Griffin was so spiteful," Threatt told me. "He cropped out Stanford's [from establishing shots of Kelly's on the show]. The buildings are literally connected. He cropped out that building for the entire length of the series. Everybody in Kansas City knew what was right next to it."

Joel Madison, the TV show's creator, denied this. "*Malcolm & Eddie* did not shoot at Kelly's but was located in a fictitious bar like Kelly's called

Kelly's," he told me. "But it had nothing to do with [Griffin] not getting booked at Stanford's."

"Joel produced that show," Emery responded. "And wrote that show. And pitched that show. And ran that show. So my opinion is, Joel will tell you what it meant. And if it meant a 'Fuck you' to Stanford's, Joel would tell you. So this is a great example of how perception is completely subjective....All the Glazers probably took it as a slight that there was no mention of their club. I imagine that take comes from the sour grapes of some rich dicks."

It's also possible the Griffin-Stanford's rivalry might be another instance of myth-making by an exaggeration-prone Craig Glazer. Especially since multiple people have told me Griffin *did* return to the club. "Three years later, after [Griffin] had made it," Marks said, "he came back and showed up in the lobby [of Stanford's]. And I said, 'Oh, here we go again.' And [he] actually apologized to me....God bless, that's thirty-five years ago, so [Griffin] might not even remember who I am anymore. Although I don't see how he could forget. I sure remembered him."

Craig pushed the Griffin rivalry in the press for years after. And while Craig might not have gotten the credit, or the big public make-up he wanted, the people in attendance at Stanford's one night in the early 2000s probably witnessed all the closure they needed and then some. "Eddie did

Kelly's Bar, 1980s. *Missouri Valley Special Collections.*

a documentary and came back and was filming everything in Kansas City," Meurrens said, referring to 2003's *Dysfunktional Family*. "And of all things, Carlos Mencia was the comic that weekend. Eddie asked if he could do a show. And the people on either [the] Friday or Saturday late show got a four-hour comedy show, because Carlos never knows when to shut the fuck up and would go for two and a half hours. And Eddie asked me if he could do fifteen, twenty minutes. And he did an hour. Because he just wanted to perform on the stage again there at Westport where he started." And I'm guessing this time he was free to say whatever motherfucking thing he wanted.

Chapter 4

THE WORST CLUB IN THE COUNTRY—THE BEST STAGE IN THE COUNTRY

While the comedy aspect of Stanford & Sons was having great success, there were various attempts at restaurant expansion by Stan, and that's when the business side of things got a little rocky. After a few very expensive failures, he was millions in debt and seemingly had burned every bridge in town—he did fuck people's wives, after all. This basically meant there was nobody left who would loan him any money. So Craig and Jeff took over the Westport location, along with all its financial problems, in 1996.

"Stan would pull up in his Jaguar with some twenty-five-year-old girl in it begging Craig for $200 so they could go do something on a Friday night," former GM Ron Meurrens told me. And when Craig and Jeff finally cut off their financially strapped father, he decided to take them to court. All Stan was asking was an allowance of $5,000 per month for life.

The spat between father and sons was messy and it was public. The sons won in court. The *Kansas City Star* called it "a tale as dark and complex as a Tennessee Williams play," in a front-page story in 2000. Going through old newspaper articles about the family drama was another wild ride, with a few unexpected twists and turns along the way.

Stan opened a rival club, which lasted about a year, and tried to lure talent away from Jeff and Craig. Then the family appears to have made up overnight. By March 2001, Craig was telling the press that he was going to run for mayor of Kansas City. While there were a thousand reasons this could and should never happen, it would have been an entertaining run nonetheless. When reporters asked Craig about the incumbent mayor Kay Barnes, he replied, "What does she know of life? I've been in jail. I've been in a gunfight. I've hung out with movie stars….I've lived life."[58]

Right on cue, Craig got busted for cocaine again. So, naturally, Stan ran for mayor in his place. Then it got leaked to the press that in 1996, Stan had been arrested for soliciting a prostitute. And it was also reported that he may have gotten those charges suspiciously dropped by County Prosecutor and future U.S. Senator Claire McCaskill.[59] He stayed in the race nonetheless.

Barbara Shelly, covering Stan's campaign for the *Kansas City Star*, wrote, "Glazer is an amusing, charismatic man with a long history of failed business and broken relationships. I watched him this week in four forums. His lack of knowledge of city issues is breathtaking." Stan would go on to get 40 percent of the vote anyway.[60]

"I was praying he'd be mayor," David Naster said. "We'd have had CNN trucks [at Stanford & Sons] every day."

Instead of getting one of the most memorable mayors in the city's history in either Craig or Stan, the most unforgettable dynamic from this era of Stanford & Sons—at least to the comics—seems to be the underhanded business practices of brothers Craig and Jeff. "Stanford's was notorious for being the shadiest club in the country," comedian Mike Baldwin told me. "I think it was good for me as a comedian because it taught me the worst parts of the business. So I wasn't surprised when similar things popped up at other clubs. I dealt with the worst, so the 'bad' weren't that bad."

"There were a lot of issues when it came to being paid correctly," comedian Johnny O said. "It was almost like they would slightly short your check just to see if you would say something."

"Craig Glazer was cheap," comedian James Inman told me. "Every single time I got paid it was a hundred or $200 less than I was supposed to get. *Every single time*. I didn't get mad. At that point, it was a 'Craig Glazer tax' that I just started accepting after a while. Because what else was I gonna do? He's got the only club in town."

"It was, like, their business model to like screw the emcee and the feature," comedian Tim Gaither said. "And the reason they did it so much is because so many comics took it."

"It was always a fight," comedian Emery Emery said. "You could get booked for $300 and watch the room fill up the entire week you're there hosting. And then [you'd] have one of the Glazers go, 'Yeah, we didn't do as well as we thought we were gonna do, so we're gonna pay you $175. That's all we can pay you.'"

Left: Tim Gaither in a recent image. *Tim Gaither.*

Right: Mike Baldwin and Nikki Glaser. *Mike Baldwin.*

"They had a whole system worked out," Baldwin said. "The owner would promise $500 for a week of shows. And payday was after the Sunday show, but the owners were never there on Sunday. So when you would complain about your $300 check to the manager, they would say, 'I don't know anything. You'll have to talk to the owners about that.' And most people would never talk to the owners about it. They had flights early on Monday, so they couldn't go back to the club to confront them about it. They did that pretty consistently the whole time I worked there. They probably saved $500 or $1,000 each month by shorting everyone a few hundred bucks."

"If we got paid," comedian Andrea Caspari said, "we had to run to the bank and see who got there first. Otherwise there wasn't enough money. So if the feature and the host got paid at the same time, we were like, 'Who goes in first? Because mine will cash and yours will bounce.'"

"One time, I remember I lost a check and they were like, 'Then it's gone,'" comedian Nikki Glaser remembered. "And I'm like, 'Is that really how it works?'…I can only imagine how much they screwed over comics through the years.…[Craig] really is, like, the archetype of the club owner that people make fun of."

Chris Porter and AJ Finney. *AJ Finney.*

"Jeff was a heroin addict," comedian Chris Porter said. "Craig surrounded himself with toxic women and cocaine and just loved that scene. He was, like, the last '80s club owner, where your check might be short, [or] he would try to pay you in cocaine. Like, all that stuff."

If all that isn't enough, there are multiple stories of Craig and Jeff getting into fistfights with each other at the restaurant during business hours. In two different stories, a comedian was offered frozen chicken wings in lieu of payment. In another story, a young Chris Porter asked Craig to watch a tape of his set and then give him feedback. So Craig responded by summoning Porter to the club after the late show on a Friday and then watching the tape with three local exotic dancers, who were instructed to give Porter their own notes on his set. This brings us to another category of Craig Glazer stories.

"Craig was always dating strippers," comedian Steve Kramer said. "Three or four at the same time."

"Craig brought strippers with him wherever he went," comedian Dean Boese agreed. "He was in his sixties…and he thought all these strippers made him The Man."

Tim Gaither in a recent image. *Tim Gaither.*

"[Craig is] an older guy with an appetite for quite younger women," journalist Hearne Christopher Jr. told *The Pitch* in 2013. "And he loves to kiss and tell."[61] And that was before the author David Hudnall also mentioned that "[Craig] maintains a rotating cast of girlfriends, all apparently comfortable with open relationships and being discussed on Johnny Dare's [radio] show."

"[Craig] had a lot of stories of doing coke and fucking girls, and he was always around with some *Playboy* playmate," Nikki Glaser said. "I mean, it all could have been an act for someone who was deeply closeted."

"He would embarrass the shit out of me," Tim Gaither said. "Like, we'd be [doing morning radio] and we'd go to breakfast and there'd be a family sitting five feet away. And just out of nowhere he's like, 'So, you ever fuck a girl in the butt?' And stuff like that. And I'd be like, 'Craig! There's a family right there, dude!' I think he was lonely."

"[Craig] always was trying to keep up this image," Justin Leon said. "And you saw it slowly deteriorating with age and how he was holding on. He was on some kind of human growth hormone or steroids for a minute. He always liked to be onstage without sleeves on his shirt."

"He would have people come to the club and inject steroids into his ass," Dean Boese said of Craig. "Like, right there in the bar [with] people around. He didn't care." Then he added, "Most of the time [at other clubs around the country], it's the comics who misbehave. You go to Kansas City, it's the owner."

It gets worse. There was also a lot of alleged racism. "You can't say Craig wasn't racist. Because he probably definitely was," Gaither said. "He'd be talking to some woman, and within two minutes he was dropping n-bombs....And then the lady would be offended because he'd said the n-word. Which she rightfully should. And he'd be like, 'What? What are you getting offended about?'"

"I definitely heard him say racist shit," Glaser said. "Where you're like, 'Oh, God. I've never even been around someone who thinks it's okay to talk like this.'"

"I came up in the worst place ever," Chris Porter said. "So now when I go to, like, the Toledo Funny Bone that everyone complains about, I'm like,

Justin Leon and AJ Finney. *AJ Finney*.

'This place is great! You have a hotel. My check's correct'…I know what it's like to be treated like a piece of dog shit."

"We got fucked over hard, all different types of ways, by the Glazer boys," Leon said. "So if a club outside of Kansas City did 75 percent of what they said they were gonna do, we were like, 'All right, that's a lot better than how the boys fuck us.'"

"No one was gonna throw anything worse at you than the Glazers did," Gaither agreed. "I remember Jeff one time saying, 'What do you do when this happens at other clubs?' I go, 'It doesn't happen at other clubs! They always give me my money.'"

"But," Mike Baldwin added, "they had packed crowds almost all the time. So it was still kind of worth the loss."

Gaither seems to agree that all the pain was worth it. "I've been doing comedy now twenty-six years, twenty-four for a living," Gaither said in 2024. "And to this day, I've never been in a better room. I mean, I headlined that room way before I was ready…just because it was so good. It could carry you. You didn't have to have headliner time to headline that room if you were funny—just because it was such a hot room. The dimensions of the room were just perfect. If you didn't do well in there, you probably weren't very funny."

"It was always packed," James Inman said. "People talk about, 'Oh, it's a notorious club.' There's clubs in [other cities] where they couldn't hardly get anybody in except on Friday and Saturday night. Craig loved comedy. I mean, yeah, he was an ex-gangster that posed as a cop and would rip off drug dealers and all that kind of stuff—and he just got out of jail. But he loved comedy."

"I'm not gonna take anything away from that room," Leon said. "I loved that room. Every other room that I've ever been in for my entire comedy career, I compare to how it feels to that room. Low ceiling. It was a small stage. It was real close. It could hold a bunch of people. And it would just explode. When that room started rocking, it was un-fucking-real. And you couldn't get that from anybody else than the Glazer boys. It was a little grimy. It was a little wannabe Hollywood. It was a little bit everything that they were."

You don't get Kansas City jazz without the corruption of political boss Tom Pendergast, who ignored Prohibition laws, which allowed for all-night jam sessions. And hey, maybe you don't get that Stanford's stage or the most infamous open mic story of all time without the equally infamous Glazer family. But before we jump back into the Kyle Parris story, there is one other infamous comedy story I need to tell you first.

Chapter 5

THE WHEELCHAIR

The only person in the world whom Kyle Parris told about his plans for the open mic was comedian Emery Emery.[62] Which actually makes a lot of sense. Emery was a twenty-year stand-up veteran at that point. He'd been a mentor to many of the younger comics in the scene. And if not for Parris and what he was about to do at Stanford's, Emery Emery would probably hold the title for the most infamous set in the history of Kansas City comedy himself. In fact, when I initially talked to comedian Paul Provenza in 2024 about the well-known Parris set, he added, "You should probably also ask Emery Emery about his story with the wheelchair."

I took Provenza's advice, and Emery explained his wheelchair saga to me over coffee in Burbank shortly after. It's a fucking doozy.

Emery began his comedy career in Kansas City in the early '80s, basically emulating comedians like Gallagher and Howie Mandel. But everything changed for him when he saw the darker social commentary of Bill Hicks. "I didn't realize I could say things that meant anything until I saw Hicks," he told[63] the *Kansas City Star* in 1996. "I never made the connection, that I could use material to get killer laughs and deliver some hard-line points of view."

In that same article, titled "If You're Not Offended, Emery Emery Hasn't Done His Job," Emery is photographed with a beard, shaggy brown hair and glasses, as well as a copy of Hunter S. Thompson's *Songs of the Doomed: More Notes on the Death of the American Dream*. He's almost presenting himself—coincidentally, he says—exactly as Bill Hicks looked in 1993, shortly before he died of pancreatic cancer. "The need to offend, to agitate and disturb, became a hunger for Emery," the article said. But Emery's masterpiece in offensiveness, agitation and disturbance at that point remained almost a decade away.

Emery's wheelchair story starts with veteran comic Chris "Crazy Legs" Fonseca, who had been born with cerebral palsy and performed using a wheelchair. "He was always really frustrated by, and struggled with, the fact that he had an obvious disability and that his act was so built around that," Emery told me of Fonseca. "Chris was frustrated by the fact that he would get standing ovations off of what even he perceived as kind of not-that-great stuff sometimes. He was frustrated that it seemed like people were more supportive of him *because* of his disability."

In an attempt to use respectful language while writing about this topic, I saw several columns and language guides mention that being referred to as "inspirational" can indeed be considered offensive to people with disabilities. According to the Stanford University language guide[64] on disabilities, "Successful disabled people should be celebrated in much the same way as successful non-disabled people are. Depicting everyone with a disability in unsophisticated, feel-good ways for touching the hearts and opening the minds of non-disabled people is both objectifying and degrading." And then it referred to this concept as "inspiration porn."

As I mentioned in the introduction of this book, the one time I saw Fonseca perform was in 2002 at the Summit in Iowa City, where he did indeed receive a standing ovation. And on his website, Fonseca mentions knowing that "it's unusual to see a handicapped person up onstage, and if I do well, the crowd may get something out of it besides the laugh. But I'm not out there on any kind of a mission to promote disabled people and demonstrate what they can or can't do. I'm a comedian, and I'm just trying to be funny."[65]

Emery Emery. *Greg Edwards.*

In addition to Fonseca, Emery also worked with comedian Paul Shryack, who also had cerebral palsy and used a wheelchair. And a *Kansas City Star* article[66] from 1998 about their friendship also mentions Shryack's standing ovations. "Paul

Shryack was also an inspiration," Emery told me. "As is my nephew Collin, who is also wheelchair bound due to muscular dystrophy. In fact, Collin was the strongest influence, because when I hung out with Collin, watching people pretend to be blind to him, not wanting to look directly at him and sometimes even getting in his way…really influenced my desire to pull off this experiment."

And what an experiment it was. Emery would conduct it on the road, on the last night of his week in whatever town he was performing. On those nights, he performed his sets from a wheelchair. "I maybe wrote four or five jokes about being in a wheelchair," he said. "But mostly, I just did my normal stand-up material."

That is, until he got to the end of his set. After doing an hour or so of stand-up, Emery would end his set with a speech where he would admonish the crowd to question everything they were told and remind them how easily people can be tricked. At the end, "I would say, 'Thank you. Good night,'" Emery said. "And then, because I gave this little inspirational speech, I would get these standing ovations that I never got as a *stand up* stand-up."

Emery told me the standing ovations came about 90 percent of the time. And he began asking himself what this all meant, how important it might be, what it said about human nature and if it was even moral to do that act at all. "Anyway, so they're applauding and they start to stand up," he continued. "And then *I'd* stand up at the end of that. And they would stop and [*gasp*]. And then they'd understand that I'd just tricked them…they'd get that I'm making a point. And it worked. It *always* worked."

Despite club managers and staff being incredibly nervous about the wheelchair act and how customers might react, according to Emery, no one ever got angry. And he did this closer for two or three years straight. "And then I didn't do [the wheelchair act] for a while," he told me. "Another year or two went by. And then I'm hanging out with [comedian] Trevor Taylor…. And we're talking about the wheelchair bit. And he goes, 'You should just pretend that you're in a wheelchair…like, totally go with it. Why didn't you go the full route?' I go, 'I should do that. That's a fucking good idea. That's very Andy Kaufman–esque, isn't it?' And he's like, 'Yeah, it is.' And I go, 'I'm gonna do that.'"

But as Emery contemplated how he could possibly pull off a stunt like this, Taylor was quick to call his bluff. "He goes, 'You're never gonna do this,'" Emery said. "And I go, 'No, I'm really serious about it.' He goes, 'You come up with ideas all the time you don't do. You're a fucking idiot. You're not gonna do it.'…He goaded me into committing to this idea. And the

Emery Emery and AJ Finney. *AJ Finney*.

way he goaded me was, he goes, 'If you're serious, launch it tonight....Let's announce it online. You were in an accident. You broke your back. Launch it tonight.'"

Amazingly, Emery agreed to go through with the plan. So that night, Taylor made an announcement on a pretty popular comedy message board detailing a very fictitious tragedy. Emery, as Taylor regretted to inform everyone, had just been in a terrible accident. He'd been test-driving a BMW in Santa Clarita, California, when he hit a patch of sand that had recently fallen off a truck, and the crash left Emery paralyzed from the waist down with a spinal cord injury. Taylor also made sure to add that Emery and the owner of the BMW had full auto insurance coverage and that Emery had very good health insurance, so he didn't need any financial help.

An experienced con man, Craig Glazer called bullshit right away. "Craig Glazer is actually really smart," comedian James Inman said. "He's got street smarts. He's like, 'I don't know, James. I don't know about this Emery thing. I don't think he's really got his back broken. It doesn't make any sense. Like, Emery doesn't have the fucking credit. They're not gonna let him test-drive a brand-new BMW—for all these reasons.' And I'm like, '*Noooo*. How can you say that, Craig? You're just an asshole.'"

"James Inman was the kind of guy that was going around passing the cup [saying,] 'We gotta make money for Emery,'" comedian Tim Gaither said. "He was pretty hurt by it."

"I mean, he fully pulled me in," Inman agreed. "For like, a long time."

"I honestly knew it was bullshit from the start," Gaither said. "Emery would look at me sometimes. And he had this look on his face like, 'You know this is bullshit, don't you?' And I'd look back at him like, 'Yes, I do.' But I wouldn't say anything....I let him have his little thing. But I knew it was bullshit."

Emery was living in Los Angeles at the time. And he lived most of his day-to-day life outside the wheelchair. But if he was going anywhere he knew he'd see another comic, he'd show up in the chair.

"He comes to town, and he's in his wheelchair," Inman said. "He had his mom drive him [to the club]. And I'm like, 'Man, this can't be true. I don't know. I've heard too much behind the scenes.' Like, people saw him running to catch a flight at an airport in L.A. and stuff. So I go there. We hang out. He's in his wheelchair. And they do the show and everything. And we're talking at the club, and I'm like, 'All right...I'm leaving, Emery.' And so I get in my car. And I drive around the building. And I'm waiting in my car to see how he gets in the car. Because I'm like, 'Surely he's not gonna keep doing this with his mom. Is he?' And sure enough, I'm watching. He rolls up to the fucking car and has his mom help him in the car. He probably suspected I'd be watching or something. So that's how far he was going with this fucking prank."

While Emery swears that he wouldn't have run through an airport, since he even traveled using the wheelchair, the rest is true. "Yes, my mother was indeed well aware of the experiment and she did help me in and out of the car when I was in Kansas City," Emery said. "It wasn't that I was worried Jim Inman would be watching me—it was that I was concerned *anybody* might catch sight of me."

"We'd all been talking about this, going, 'Someone needs to fucking just stab him in the leg with a knife.'" Inman continued. "Because if he flinches, we know he doesn't have his back broken." When I asked why no one ever did, he replied, "Because what if he's really paralyzed?" And—fair enough.

Only a handful of comics were in-the-know about this not being on the level. That list included Provenza, who wound up hiring Emery to edit his 2005 documentary *The Aristocrats* because of it. The irony is that working on that film wound up delaying Emery's chance to finally reveal his big secret. "I was planning on doing it for the one year [anniversary]," Emery said. "But I got stuck in a room with Provenza...and couldn't find an escape route."

Emery had been turning down paid work because he didn't think it was right to accept money while he pretended to have a disability. But he would perform on free shows and fundraisers without feeling guilty. That was the code. And if he could only manage to get himself booked on a big fundraiser of some sort, he could finally reveal everything and then move on with his life.

That chance came on October 24, 2004, at the Uptown Theater in Kansas City—two years to the day of Emery's fake accident.[67] Comedian A. Whitney Brown from *Saturday Night Live* and *The Daily Show* was in town along with Boston comedy legend Barry Crimmins for an event to raise money for Democratic candidates, specifically former Mayor Emanuel Cleaver in his first bid to represent Missouri's Fifth Congressional District in Washington, D.C.

"When we got to the theater, I'm in the wheelchair," Emery said. "We're all sitting around. And A. Whitney Brown is…kinda holding court with all these younger comics. And everybody's really excited to be hanging out with what turned out to be just a crabby asshole.…We're all liberals in that room. So we're all in agreement. But when someone would say something, he would condescendingly attack some aspect of what we were talking about. Every single moment in that room was like that. Until I asked a question."

Emery resented, and seemingly still resents, being treated differently by Brown—allegedly—because of his perceived disability. "He's capable of being nice to the guy in the wheelchair," Emery said. "No one else in that room got the behavior that I got from him. He was pleasant. He was supportive. He was sweet. He was kind. It was amazing…and horrific."

Those feelings were about to become mutual once Emery got on stage. "At the end of my act," Emery said, "I said, 'Ladies and gentlemen, we've had a great time here tonight. And thank you for fundraising for the Democrats. I'm proud to be part of this. I do want to say something from a bipartisan standpoint. And that is, regardless of how you vote, regardless of who you vote for, whether they're Republican, Independent, Democrat, Green—I don't care. Whoever you vote for, watch them and watch them like a hawk. They are liars. And they will trick you. And when they start doing the things they didn't say they were gonna do, and when they don't fulfill the promises they said they were gonna fulfill, when [you] discover that they've deceived you, vote them out. Don't just vote your party. Vote out the liars. Because it's easy to be deceived. You can be looking at someone and think they are one thing, and they are just *not*. They are another. Don't fall for that shit. Thank you very much.'"

As comedian and witness Elliott Threatt put it, "He was better than Tom Cruise in *Born on the Fourth of July*." After Emery said goodnight, the Uptown

Theater crowd began to give him a standing ovation. Just like he'd planned. And as soon as they did, Emery also got up out of his wheelchair and stood right along with them.

The clapping halted immediately. Everyone in the room collectively stopped and gasped for air, all at the same time. "If I was wearing a tie," Emery told me, "the gasp would have caused it to leave my chest and go toward the audience....I mean, it was *guttural*. The whole room was like, '*What*?!?'"

"And then the gasp dissipated," he told me. "And then the applause *erupted*....They got it. They connected with it. They processed it....It was amazing. It was the best moment, up to that point, in my life. And I have a daughter."

Obviously, not everyone in attendance was happy with Emery's stunt. "We're just all shocked," Threatt said. "[Like,] 'What the *fuck*?!?' And then A. Whitney's so pissed off, [he] says 'I can't believe that! I offered you *compassion*!'" And that's when, according to Emery and Threatt, A. Whitney Brown spat in Emery's face.

"I couldn't believe [it]," Threatt told me. "[Brown] was so gentle. But it offended him so much, he spit in Emery Emery's face. That's how fucking crazy it was. He spit in his face right in front of everybody."

"He goes, 'That's not comedy,'" Emery said. "'Nothing about that is comedy. It's not funny. It's not fucking comedy. You're not a comedian. It's not fucking funny. You're a piece of shit.' I'm paraphrasing."

The next day, Brown was on Threatt's *All Comedy Radio* on 1340 KCKN to discuss the previous night's event.[68] Emery sent me a copy of the recording. When the topic came up, Brown said that Emery had done his wheelchair stunt in front of the wrong guy. "I felt personally abused," he told Threatt, "because, okay, if you're gonna do that as an act, *fine*. But he put on that act to me, personally, up in the office [before the show]. And that, to me, is just lying....The worst part is, I think he's trying to elicit sympathy. And he will then criticize you for giving him sympathy. It's like, 'I got you to give me sympathy to show that you treat people in a wheelchair differently. Now I'm gonna make fun of you for that.'"

"He's not really in a wheelchair," Threatt replied. "So who is he to speak on behalf of the wheelchair people?"

"My point exactly," Brown said. "And he says he's writing a book about his experiences in a wheelchair. Don't you think somebody who's *really* in a wheelchair should write that book? Does he want to take that away from them too?"

"*Black Like Me* written by Billy Graham," Threatt joked.

"*Lame Like Me*," Brown responded. "That's his act. It was offensive, I thought. I felt it was quite offensive."

Listening to the recording now, there was something very funny to me about comedians in 2004 finding something offensive beyond the pale just six minutes after a co-host used the terms "butch dyke" and "men with boobs" to refer to women he'd seen at a recent Indigo Girls concert and no one batted an eye. They also riffed some same-sex marriage jokes that I'm guessing none of these guys would even think about repeating now. But somehow the wheelchair thing justified spitting in another man's face?

The recording (and logic) proves that a whole lot can change in twenty years. As I said before, that line often moves. It's the thing every comedian dances around in their own time and place. As Darren Bodeker said in my previous book, "[Just] being a comedian, you have to go across that line into the devil's territory. And the devil ain't got no ideology but the devil, bro."

Yes, times change, and so do people and attitudes and political climates. And I realize Threatt and Brown had just done a fundraiser for the Democratic Party the night before, so they were ostensibly as progressive as two straight guys could be in America in 2004. But I'm just saying that the outrage over one thing but not the other reads as kinda funny in 2025.

Threatt, by the way, seems to have a good sense of humor about the whole thing now. "The older I get," he told me, "The more hilarious [I find it that Emery] drove a guy who was like Mother Theresa to spit on him. I mean, I was pissed at the time. I've since seen [Emery] and talked to him and everything—*of course*. We're cool."

As for Emery, he took the Brown interaction as a personal victory. "Dude, he was the bow tie on the whole experiment," he said.

All of this, I want to remind you, occurred three years *after* the Kyle Parris incident we're about to discuss, even though Emery's "test run" of wheelchair shows had happened in the years prior. That being said, I do find it interesting that the guy who would fake his own paralysis and commit to the bit for *two full years*—and told me in 2024 he has zero regrets about doing so—would also be the only person in the world to have pre-knowledge of Parris's plan and the most infamous open mic set of all time.

And still, his response to Parris was especially telling. "I said, 'Don't do it,'" he told me. "This is crazy."

Chapter 6

THE 'POSSUM

Kyle Parris made a list of all the items he'd need for his big open mic performance at Stanford's. He got a towel, dishwashing gloves, a hula hoop, his vacuum cleaner and his trusty red Igloo cooler, which he'd lined with trash bags. Then he put on a jacket and tie, with jeans instead of dress pants, and loaded all the props into his blue Dodge Caravan. On the way to the club, Parris realized that he'd forgotten to buy ice for the cooler, but as he tells it, it was too late for him to go back for ice or stop anywhere to buy it. Especially now that he had roadkill to find.

At the time, Parris was living in Warrensburg, Missouri, a fifty-mile commute to Westport on U.S. Highway 50. And on that drive, he started looking for dead animals. "This is Missouri," he said. "There's a lot of roadkill."

The first two times Parris pulled over were unsuccessful. "One time it was a dead cat and it was too mangled up, so I couldn't use it," Parris said. "And I pulled over again. It was another dead animal. I forgot what it was, but it was too mangled up. It was in half. I can't do that. So the third time was the charm."

Halfway to the club, Parris found a dead 'possum he deemed suitable. Although at the time, he thought it was a ferret. "I didn't know my animals from a hole in the ground," he told me. Regardless, he took out his dishwashing gloves, stuffed the animal into the trash-lined cooler, loaded it back into his van and made his way to Stanford's for their standard pre-show meeting with all the comics.

For Andrea Caspari, this particular night made a huge impression—not only because of the events that were about to happen but also because it happened to be her first open mic in Kansas City. She was coming into the situation completely blind. Before the show, according to Caspari, twenty-five to thirty comedians crowded into the basement of the club so the new comics could learn the running order and the rules—comics get three minutes, and a light will come from the back of the room telling them when it's time to wrap up. That sort of thing. And to the best of her recollection, Parris drew no. 3 in the running order, and she drew no. 5.

"I [was] just trying to soak it all in," Caspari remembered. "I don't know anybody. I'm one of very few women. But I see this really odd, super tall, really angular, crazy-looking guy. And his hair was very poofy at the time…and kind of a longer nose, little weasel teeth. Let's just not—he's a strange looking dude.…And I see that he has an Igloo cooler with him."

That cooler, by the way, was well known in the Kansas City comedy community already. "For a long time," comedian Chris Porter said, "every Thanksgiving, Kyle would come in with a full turkey. His big schtick was he had a [public access] show. That was his premise for every bit."

"We didn't have YouTube yet," Parris explained. "We had public access." So in this public access–themed bit, Parris would introduce himself as the host of a cooking show. And then he would say something to the effect of, "Every Thanksgiving, we cook turkeys for our families. But our most important family members get left out. And I'm talking about our pets. So tonight I'm going to show you how to make a wonderful Thanksgiving turkey for your pet."

Kyle Parris. *Greg Edwards.*

And that's when Parris brought out a thawed turkey from his cooler and placed it on a baking tray on top of the stool. He would then pull out a can of dog food, eat a little bit of it with his hands and

Andrea Caspari in a recent image. *Andrea Caspari.*

then stuff the dog food inside the raw turkey. Then he would take out cat food and do the same thing. "Which grossed people out and made some people laugh," Parris told me. "That was part of the joke."

"Now, I want to make sure that the dog food and cat food are deep enough inside the turkey that it bastes in all the turkey juices and increases the flavor," he would tell the probably disgusted audience. And then Parris, only making matters worse, would pull out a dildo and proceed to push it in and out of the turkey, playing it deadpan as if it were a normal kitchen tool. "Like they do in *Airplane!*," he explained—also with a straight face. Then he would take the dildo out of the turkey and lick it as if were a wooden spoon.

"Describing it, it doesn't do it justice," Porter assured me. "It was hilarious."

I'll take his word for it. This *was* an annual tradition at Stanford's for years, after all. A description of the act actually made it into the *Kansas City Star* on August 11, 2000 (which also means he didn't just save the bit for Thanksgivings). The reporter hilariously described the dildo as a "marital aid," in case you were wondering. "At the very least," the article also said, "Parris shouldn't have any trouble making audiences remember him."[69]

"Every time he got up there, you knew that something weird was gonna happen," comedian Tom Becka said. "Not your standard stand-up by any stretch of the imagination."

"Comics loved Kyle," comedian Dean Boese said. "And I think Kyle's a goddamned genius....But audiences don't always get him. And certainly not in a comedy club setting. He just scared people a lot of the time."

Over the years, Parris had other well-known bits involving this Igloo cooler. For another oft-mentioned act, he would wear nothing but women's underwear, climb a stool and then jump into a pile of "five or six" pies—which also emerged from the cooler. "I just writhed around in the pies," Parris explained. "And I got up and slipped. Got up again, slipped. And I had chocolate cake hanging off my ass so it looked like a turd coming out."

So *yeah*, the comics definitely knew this cooler pretty well. "If he brought a cooler," Porter said, "you knew it was *on*."

Aware of this, after the pre-show meeting, Parris decided to put the cooler back in his van for the time being. He wanted his big act to be a surprise. At this point, it's probably important to remind you that this was July in Kansas City and could have been over ninety degrees that day. As baseball great Ichiro Suzuki famously told Bob Costas in 2003, "August in Kansas City is hotter than two rats in a fucking wool sock."[70] Well, July in Kansas City is even hotter than August. And probably much hotter inside in the van, where there was no ice in the cooler.

The show started around 8:30 p.m. So Parris also had time to hide his vacuum cleaner onstage behind a curtain before people started coming in. The size of the crowd varies wildly in people's memories, so it depends on who you ask. Caspari and comedian Amie Clark believe that the club was full that night, which would have been roughly 265 people.[71] But Caspari concedes it may have only *felt* full because of her first-time jitters. "It's very possible there were only, like, 80 people," she said.

Tim Gaither guessed there were "at least one hundred people" there that night, including staff and comics. Tom Becka remembers something in the seventy-five to one hundred range, while Porter guessed somewhere between fifty and sixty. A comedian named Grey and club manager Ron Muerrens also guessed around fifty. I've heard Parris guess there were thirty to forty people. I've also heard him say there were just under one hundred. The lowest number I've heard is from comedians Boese and Johnny O, who both guessed only fifteen people were in attendance. But again, with up to thirty comics on the lineup, plus Stanford's staff, it seems like fifty might be decent guess. Either way, it was an intimate club, which gave it the *feeling* of being packed. But, as we'll see later, there was definitely room to move.

Wherever Parris was in the lineup (we'll just assume he was no. 3), he knows that when only two comics were in front of him, he went back out to the van to retrieve his cooler. When he opened the van, Parris remembers smelling the outside of the cooler to see if there was an odor. Since there wasn't, he assumed everything was fine and dandy, went back upstairs with the cooler in tow and waited by the side stage until he was introduced.

"I had my suit on," Parris told me. "I had the cooler in my lap. And the hula hoop. And my gloves on top of the cooler. The host was a friend of mine named Dean Boese. And when he was announcing me, he was like, 'Oh, ladies and gentlemen, comics in the back, guess what—Kyle Parris has a cooler!'"

"We're like, '*Yes*! All right!" Porter said.

"I'm watching like a spectator," Caspari said, "[thinking], 'What's this weird guy gonna do?'"

After the introduction, an extremely nervous Parris walked onstage and laid the towel down over the stool. Next, as he described it to me, "I said, 'Hey, I'm Kyle Parris and I'm an animal trainer. And I got this ferret with me. And we're gonna do some tricks for you.'" And just as a fun bit of side detail, comedian and witness Amie Clark remembers Parris referring to his animal as "Mr. Jingles."

That's when Parris first opened the air-tight cooler and was knocked back, not only by the pungent stench of death it released but also by the heat coming off the decomposing 'possum. "I opened it up and the heat in that place went up, like, ten degrees, I'm not even kidding," Parris said.[72] "Then there was the *stench*. But I'm a professional. I'm gonna go through with it."

Top: Amie Clark in a recent image. *Amie Clark.*

Bottom: Tom Becka. *Tom Becka.*

Parris was not the only person who began suffering. The front row began covering their mouths and noses, reacting audibly in disgust to whatever the fuck was in that cooler. Parris has said he could see their eyes watering within seconds. And that's when he reached in, retrieved the body of the dead animal and set it on the stool. "By this point, the stink had hit the second row," he told me.

Tom Becka was the next comedian due up and had a visceral reaction when I reminded him of the story twenty-three years later. "Now I'm gonna be sick," he winced, before adding, "When he picked it up, there was juices and shit that drained on the floor. Oh, God, yeah, I'm not gonna sleep tonight."

Chris Porter was at a table in the back of the room with other comedians when the 'possum was revealed. "We're in the back going, 'Is that real?'" he told me. But then, "the people in the front row immediately started to vacate....And when we saw [people get up], we were like, '*Probably real.*'... And you see blood drip from the mouth of this fucking dead 'possum, and we're all in the back like, 'Oh, it's *real*!'"

Going along with the bit as written, Parris exclaimed, "Oh, my God! My ferret is choking!" And then he retrieved his hidden vacuum cleaner from behind a curtain.

And I just want to say that no matter how many times I've heard or thought about this story, the fact that he used a vacuum cleaner at all for the next part of the performance will forever boggle my mind. "He pulls out this vacuum," Porter said, "shoves the nozzle down the gullet of the beast and flips this thing on."

"A lot of people don't know this," Porter continued. "When a vacuum sucks, it also blows it out somewhere. [So] the odor from within this rotting animal is now being expelled at 110 volts throughout this entire comedy [club]."

Over the years, I'd heard that Parris had rigged the vacuum to blow air out instead of suck air in. And a lot of witnesses told me the same thing. But that isn't the case—not that there's much of a distinction between the two in what actually happened that night. "Immediately," Boese told me, "a cloud of stench explodes out of this thing, [and] wafts through the comedy club."

"You can see as the death smell rolls throughout the front of the room," comedian Justin Leon said.

My comedian friend Brendan McGowan said it was "not unlike the Ark of the Covenant being opened [in *Raiders of the Lost Ark*], and the souls of the [conquered] people begin killing Nazis."

"All the orifices of our beings were filled with dead 'possum bloat," Clark said. "[Stanford & Sons] was like a fire box. Up a set of stairs. Only one exit. I don't think any windows. And restrooms in the back, thank God. But there's no good air exchange in this space. It is a trapped space." And once it hit them, all hell broke loose.

"Some people couldn't breathe and were coughing," comedian Tim Gaither said.

"People started running to the bathroom," Parris said. "[Yelling,] 'Oh my fucking God!'"

"It's like a bomb had dropped," Leon said. "Everybody is running for their lives and kinda stumbling and running down the stairs."

"We ran out like there was a fire," Porter agreed.

"There were pockets in the room you could try to retreat to that might allow you to survive," Emery Emery said.

"Tables literally were lifted and flipped," Clark said. "And I'm running to the smoking section like, 'Light all the cigarettes! Just blow it in my face! Please, God!'"

"I ran to the green room," Emery said, "We barricaded it so people couldn't come through and let [the smell] in."

"Everyone's freaking out," Caspari said. "People are running. Half the place clears out. They either leave or go to the toilets to vomit."

"At least three people were actually sick," Johnny O said.

"About three rows back is a pregnant woman," Boese said. "She gets a face full of this stench, runs for the restroom—puking so loudly we can hear her. And this is some distance away....Everybody else is running out of the club." Kansas City, it might be fun to mention now, is also known as the City of Fountains.

The pregnant woman in question, by the way, was a friend of Clark's who said she didn't go back to another comedy show again until Nate Bargatze came to the City of Fountains in 2024. And she definitely wasn't the only one traumatized.

"My father was there to see me and was in the front row," Grey told me. "I think he has comedy PTSD now. He still talks about it. Says it's the grossest thing he'd ever seen. I'm sure it blossomed into some type of phobia of roadkill and/or comedians." Then she added, "My father was an ass. To be honest, he deserved to be front and center for this."

The club's manager, Ron Meurrens, who told me he hated open mic night anyway, was in his office when he heard the commotion. "I just heard screaming," he told me, "and I heard a table get knocked over. And in the time it takes to get out of my chair and jump up to see what's going on, you could already smell this dead 'possum going through my comedy club....I get to the door and Kyle's still unhooking the 'possum from the vacuum cleaner."

Left: Andrea Caspari in a recent image. *Andrea Caspari.*

Right: Bob Saget and Ron Meurrens. *Ron Meurrens.*

That's about the time a woman vomited right in front of Meurrens. And he just saw red. According to Emery, Meurrens was a ticking time bomb back then anyway. And the comics who hadn't already fled the room were about to see his biggest explosion ever. "I'm not gonna lie to you," Meurrens told me, "not that I was the biggest Kyle Parris fan in the world anyway, [but] I lost it. I started screaming '*I'm gonna fucking kill you*!'"

"He comes out of the back," Boese said of Meurrens, "grabs me by the shirt [and says,] 'Dean, get him off stage! Get him out of here and tell him he's banned!'"

Amazingly, while all this was happening, Parris was still fully committing to the bit, trying to make it all work. "He's just looking around like, 'But wait. There's *more*,'" Clark said.

"Nobody was listening by that point," Baldwin said.

With nobody wanting to go near the stage, the comic's time-to-get-off-the-stage light was being frantically waved at Parris from the back. So Parris decided against throwing the animal through the hoop against the back wall. "There was blood coming out of the mouth and shit," Parris told me. "So I just went straight to the ending."

It's probably for the best. "I picked up a pint glass and launched it at the fucking stage and missed his head, I'd guess, by barely a foot," Meurrens remembered. "And I'm screaming, 'If I get to you, you're fucking dead!'"

With all this chaos and carnage, flipped tables, broken glass, threats of murder and actual vomit all around him, Parris said goodnight to what was left of the trapped or stampeded Stanford's crowd, and then he still *grabbed the late Mr. Jingles's paw and made it wave goodbye to the audience*. Retelling that part of the story makes Parris chuckle all these years later. But not necessarily at the right part. "The 'possum's tongue was hanging out its mouth," he laughed.

When the act was over, being as sanitary as he could possibly be, all things considered, Parris dumped the 'possum corpse, as well as the towel and the gloves, back into his cooler and closed it up tight. The new plan was to get that cooler, its contents and its stench out of the club as quickly as possible. But in the process, Parris moved the mic stand back into place for the next comedian. Which, I mean, the consideration and stage etiquette in that moment also blows my mind. But it wasn't appreciated in the moment. "As soon as he saw me touch the mic stand," Parris said, "[the next comic, Tom Becka] yelled out at the top of his lungs, '*What the fuck is he doing*?! *Oh my God*!'"

"I wasn't thrilled," Becka agreed.

"And I get it," Parris said. "He was not thinking straight. So he knew there was blood and germs and all kinds of shit on my hands. Although there wasn't—[all that] was on my gloves, which I took off."

Parris's immediate concerns were probably askew. "It was literally an emergency situation," Meurrens said. "People were trying to find a way out of this comedy club [by] any means possible because of this. And most made it to that back entrance, which was a back hallway to a radio station, and down to a parking garage. And that's the way Kyle decided to flee to get away from me."

Parris rushed the "hot cooler of death" (as Clark called it) out the back of the club. "People parted for me like the Red Sea," Parris remembered. He went down the back stairs, across the street and threw the trash bag with the animal, along with the towel and the gloves, into the nearest dumpster. And then he put the cooler back in his van. "The cooler itself was fine," Parris assured me. "It wasn't all that bad."

Meanwhile, Meurrens was still trying to find and then murder Parris. "I do remember Tom [Becka] trying to hold me back," Meurrens said. "I tried to chase [Parris] down. And I'm screaming, 'You are never setting fucking foot into my comedy club again!' And I tried to find him on the street. And I did ban him for life."

"I've never seen [Meurrens] more pissed," Dean Boese said. "Because it created a headache for him. Like, if it got out [that] Stanford's had this crazy comic do this thing, the boys would not have been happy—and that would be Craig and Jeff Glazer. So Ron was just trying to make sure that this didn't turn into a public relations nightmare."

All this probably happened in under three minutes. And still, after all this chaos, the show somehow still went on. And when I asked why on earth they would continue, everyone familiar with Stanford's reacted like I'd just asked the dumbest question in the world. "Obviously checks hadn't been dropped yet," Porter explained.

"There were bills that hadn't been paid," Caspari agreed. "You're so naïve thinking the Glazers are gonna stop. The thing [could be] on fire, but we still have checks getting to the tables."

"It's an open mic night," Porter added, "so you still have ten other comics that want to go up."

"That place probably smelled a little bad anyway," Caspari added.

So, after Parris's set, the staff got to work putting things back in order. "I turned the thermostat way down so it'd suck all the air out," said that night's bartender, Keith Ranney. "And we opened the back door, put a fan there. But I mean, it was pretty horrendous."

"Ron was like, 'Well, we gotta finish the show,'" Boese said. "And so I'm up there trying to figure out how we're going to do it when I am joined onstage by a comic named DC Young and, I believe, Keith Ranney. And they're both equipped with these industrial cans of Lysol, and they're just spraying everything down."

"I just figured [I'd] sanitize everything up there," Ranney explained. "I sanitized the seat where he sat the cooler and figured 'Why not do the microphone too?'"

"Keith is a great guy," Meurrens laughed. "If Keith was actually cleaning something, it was a first, because God knows he never cleaned his bar."

"A door opens to pretend to ventilate the space," Clark remembered. "They reset the tables, scoot [them] in, [and said,] 'Sorry about that, folks.'"

About thirty minutes after Parris's set, Dean Boese was tasked with restarting the show. Which he did in a hurry. "I went up and I specifically [said], 'Kyle Parris, ladies and gentlemen!'" Boese told me. "'And a round of applause for our Lysol gentlemen, Keith and DC.' And I brought up the next person. There was no way you were gonna do well in that moment.... It still smells like roadkill and knock-off brand Lysol as well. It's just this miasma that's sort of floating out there." But he said Becka was a pro, and he trusted him to get the room back.

Man, I would not want to be Tom Becka in that situation. Or Dean Boese, for that matter. And I especially do not envy Andrea Caspari. Other than, you know, the fact that they all have a phenomenal story to tell for the rest of their lives. They'd just seen and smelled the craziest goddamn thing to ever happen onstage at an open mic. Or possibly in any room with any mic. And now they have to recover the show or, in Caspari's case, perform their first ever open mic set in a new city. "I just am like, 'What do I do?'" Caspari said. "Thank God I wasn't next."

"The stench is still up there onstage," Becka said. "So I'm up there and I'm, like, gagging while I'm doing the damn thing. I won't say that I killed. But I at least got them focused and laughing a little bit."

When I reminded Becka that Caspari went up directly after him and that it was her first open mic in Kansas City, he had a good chuckle. "I love open mic nights," he said. "They're poetry, aren't they?"

The main thing that was still killing Caspari twenty-three years later was that she never addressed the roadkill incident at all during her set. "Can you imagine," she asked me. "You [just] do the act? I was just like,

Andrea Caspari in a recent image. *Andrea Caspari.*

'Hello everybody. My name is Andrea,' like this hadn't just happened and that thirty people weren't left watching like, sicked out. Even the people that *didn't* leave were grossed out. The stench of death was just permeating that place."

"Actually," Boese remembered, "[Caspari] did okay considering. Nobody was going to do well. Kyle had made sure of that."

Over time, patrons and comics started trickling back into the showroom from the downstairs bar. Porter remembers being shocked, turning to another comedian and saying, "Fucking nobody left. Everyone's back.'"

Everyone, that is, except for Kyle Parris. As he tried to reenter the club, he was stopped by another comic who informed him that people in the showroom had vomited, that Meurrens had banned him from Stanford's for life and wanted to murder him. "They tell me his face was so red with anger that he probably would have beat the shit out of me," Parris said. "But here's the problem—my vacuum was still onstage."

Oh yes, the fucking vacuum. The instrument of destruction itself was left at the scene of the crime. And so Parris decided to wait until someone could retrieve it for him. He sat alone, outside, on the back stairs of the club, while his performance adrenaline dissipated and the reality of his situation slowly started sinking in. When he'd been onstage and in the spotlight, he didn't realize that people in the audience were getting sick. "As soon as I heard that, my heart sank," Parris remembered. "And on top of that, I know I'm banned for life. Which I knew I deserved."

"You know, Kyle's a very sensitive dude," Porter said. "He's a very emotional guy. And he's easily affected. And so Ron screamed at him and yelled at him. And for someone like Kyle who is such a sweet soul, I'm sure that was devastating."

"I really didn't think [the 'possum] was gonna stink as bad as it [did]," Parris explained. "I knew there might be a chance. But I didn't realize just how horrible that smell was gonna be."

"He was out on the corner, like, crying," Gaither said. "That open mic was his whole life. And I was like, 'Dude, you're fine. They're not gonna ban you. They say that shit all the time.'"

The image of an emotionally shattered Kyle Parris on the back steps of Stanford's waiting for his vacuum cleaner is something that has stuck with the comics who witnessed it. And the initial version of the Parris story I heard years ago included a part where he looks up at someone and says, "I just really thought it would *work*." Which is probably just a comic's embellishment. But it actually seems to reflect Parris's thinking.

"He was hurt," Boese said. "I mean, he did not intend to do what he did. That was clear. And he absolutely was kind of broken, because he knew it was gonna cause him problems with the club."

As Parris grew increasingly distraught on the stairs, he convinced himself that his comedy career was over. Or that he could be in trouble legally—this was still a restaurant, after all. But an hour or so later, as the show was letting out, Parris could see and hear audience members leaving Stanford's. And according to Parris, the first audience member to come outside asked, "What happened to the 'possum guy?"

When audience members saw Parris on the stairs, they started walking toward him. And much to his surprise, they weren't angry. "They said, 'Dude, that was awesome!'" Parris told me. "And I think they could just tell how dejected I was....This is the weirdest compliment I've ever gotten in my whole entire twenty-five years-plus doing comedy. People came up to me and said, 'You made me vomit, but it was awesome.'"

"The only guy that lit into me," Parris continued, "was [Tom Becka]. He read me the riot act, as was his right. I get it. He came up and said, 'What the fuck was that?!?' And for the next five minutes he just ranted to me like, 'I had to worry about my own health! I had to worry about getting the audience back on track....What the fuck were you thinking?!? You're fucked! You're fucked in this town! Your career is fucking over!'"

"He didn't quite understand why he was banned from Stanford's," Becka remembered. "Emotions were high after [his set]. I liked the kid. He was a nice kid. But you can't have dead animals that might give off rabies onstage."

When the show was over, a comedian finally brought Parris his vacuum. "He didn't know what to say," Parris told me, before adding, "That was the longest drive home after a show."

When Parris got home, he disinfected his cooler and vacuum cleaner hose as best he could. And then he just kinda went on with his life. The next night, he headed back out to another open mic—away from Stanford's—where he was obviously the talk of the scene. "I started hearing all the stories about what happened the night before," Parris said. "[The comics] were not mad at all. They were actually laughing about it. Like, they were telling me stories, like people vomited on the floor, then slipped on their own vomit. Which still makes me laugh."

Everyone, it seems, was loving it. "I said, 'Was that the first 'possum you saw on your way to the club?'" Leon remembered asking Parris. "He said, 'No, I stopped at three different carcasses, but they weren't funny.'"

With the story spreading, and comedians willing to forgive so quickly or even celebrating what he did, Parris called the club to apologize. But it didn't really help his situation with the salty GM—at least for the time being. "We had to spend a few hundred dollars trying to get the smell out," Meurrens explained. "There's no windows in this place and hardly anything for ventilation. We had the worst time in the world trying to get that cleaned. I mean, I think they brought in a ServiceMaster team. But it still smelled like dead 'possum on Wednesday. It took a good week to get out. Even Craig backed me that [Parris] was banned for life for that shit."

Several of the comics from the scene were adamantly against the banishment. And a few of them began pleading Parris's case to Meurrens by saying how bad Parris felt about the whole thing. "I did not give a fuck," Meurrens told me. "I'm gonna point blank tell you, I did not care. And I sat my whole staff and every comic down in that place and told them—'If any one of you ever bring Kyle Parris into this club, you will never work in my club again. Or set foot in it.' I told my staff, 'If I am ever gone on vacation, if I ever have a day off, and I find out that one of you let Kyle Parris in? You are fucking fired.'"

Nevertheless, the comics persisted. "Everybody sincerely liked Kyle," Boese said. "And the word everybody had was that Kyle didn't think what happened was gonna happen, that he [just] hadn't thought it through."

"I think he generally thought in cartoon ideas," Grey said. "Not on the same plane as us."

"He was just pure at heart," Leon agreed. "*And* demented."

"People would ask me for months if Kyle was supposed to come back," Meurrens said, "and I was like, 'Fuck no, he cannot come back. I'm still alive.'"

But after only six months, Meurrens finally relented. "There was no official word saying that 'Your ban is officially six months,'" Parris told me. "It just turned out I waited for about six months to make an attempt to go back."

Maybe half a year was enough time for the angry parties to calm down. Maybe all the drugs floating around the club drowned out the memory, or at least the anger, from that night. Maybe it was the fact that, I don't know, fucking 9/11 happened just two months after Parris's set and probably put a few "life" things into perspective for everybody involved. But whatever the reason, Parris came back to Stanford's in early 2002. And he returned wearing one of his best jokes yet. "When he came back," Porter told me, "he was in a white T-shirt that, in marker, he had written, 'NO DEAD POSSUM.'"

Even Ron Meurrens seemed to get a genuine, if not reluctant, kick out of hearing about that shirt all these years later. And after a while, he admitted, "That's the first time I've laughed at anything Kyle Parris has said or done."

Parris's triumphant return only added to his legend. "It was definitely the story of the decade in the Kansas City comedy scene," Mike Baldwin said.

"It definitely spread around the scene," Grey said. "Everyone told newbies about it."

"What is so sad," Caspari said, "[is that] this was all…pre-camera phone. Could you imagine how viral and how famous he would be? You'd have all these reaction shots and it would go viral. I mean, you've seen Matt Rife."

Chapter 7

FAME

One of the newbie comics who heard the Kyle Parris 'possum story was Nikki Glaser, who arrived to Stanford's as a University of Kansas student two years later. "[The story] is so ingrained in my memory that I feel like I almost was there for it," she told me. And then she added, "I vividly remember him stuffing a raw turkey onstage, on a stool, and like, violating it with a dildo. I remember *that* a lot."

I interviewed Glaser in July 2024, a day before she received an Emmy nomination for her HBO/Max comedy special *Some Day You'll Die*. And one month before the *Los Angeles Times* called her "the hottest name in comedy."[73] It was also just two months after her seemingly career-defining performance on Netflix's *Roast of Tom Brady*. The roast, which took place in front of more than nine thousand people at the Kia Forum in Inglewood, California, during the Netflix Is a Joke Festival, received massive ratings on the streamer and generated headlines for days after. Much of the talk was about Glaser herself.[74]

Jason Zinoman from the *New York Times* called her performance an "absolute highlight that laid waste to everyone onstage," and *Deadline* called it "one of the most ruthlessly funny segments of a roast in years" and added, "This is the kind of moment that turns comedians into TV and movie stars."[75] As she ended her set, and the arena crowd stood in appreciation, the night's celebrity host, Kevin Hart, said, "For those that are watching at home, this is live, and that was a standing ovation. And well fucking deserved. *Well* deserved. Goddamn, Nikki." And yeah, she fucking crushed that shit.

Nikki Glaser. *Nikki Glaser.*

Two decades earlier, back when Brady had only one Super Bowl ring, Glaser was just a timid KU student making the forty-minute trek from Lawrence to Stanford's at the Hooters Plaza in Overland Park and hanging in the same bizarre comedy orbit as Kyle Parris. "I remember he was just a nice guy," Glaser said. "And quiet.... Like, he wasn't someone that you would be scared to approach offstage. He was just very soft spoken. And seemed like kind of a dork and really gracious and nice, like, 'Good set, Nikki.' I can remember him being really sweet."

It might have been his gentle demeanor that led the scene to, as Glaser put it, "keep tolerating his antics every week." Or it might have been that the Kansas City scene, in general, might have had an affinity for the outrageous, at least back then. "I look back on how I started, and even how I am now," Glaser said, "and it's, like, everyone was filthy. Like, you had to just be disgusting to get any kind of laughs. And the grosser and more dark and depraved, the better. I felt kind of poisoned by it when I left, but I do have that undertone always locked in me. That's where you go if you have nowhere else to go, is just go gross. And go shocking."

Sounds like the type of skillset that would make someone, I don't know, have a very successful set on a high-profile roast of a celebrity athlete. That and writing ability, obviously. So another big development for Glaser came after the advice she received at the time from comedian Chris Porter. "He was, like, the big man on campus," Glaser said. "I didn't even talk to him when I started doing open mics there. I was so scared of him because he was just the coolest guy. And he would just come in, do a set and then sit in the back and maybe, like, smoke cigarettes and hold court in the back—but not really watch. And I remember one night he was like, 'Glaser!' And I was like, '*Yes*???' And I walked over. He goes, 'Tell. The joke.' And I was like, 'I don't know [what you mean].' He goes, '*Tell.* The joke! Stop talking. Too much setup. *Tell. The joke.*' And that changed a lot of me. Because I was just too much setup, too much talking."

Porter feels flattered by the suggestion that he changed Glaser's comedy but slightly disagrees with her assessment. "I didn't change Nikki's comedy," he said. "She always has had a very funny mind—that was obvious from the beginning. All I did was give her some advice about how to make that funny mind shine. She took it from there. But the talent was obvious from the beginning. I am beyond proud of her and all she's accomplished. If she says that I had some small part in helping her rocket to the stratosphere, then that is an honor of the highest caliber."

The first person in that stratospheric rise to give her any work was Stanford & Sons' own Craig Glazer. "I noticed her right away because her name was Glaser," Craig said in a 2016 YouTube video.[76] "But she spelled it with an S instead of a Z. And she did open mic and I watched her. And she was very funny. And I thought, 'This girl could make it.' She was kind of a young Ellen DeGeneres."

The Ellen comparison, which Craig repeated often, was always odd to Glaser. But then again, she found a lot of things odd about Craig. "I thought he was a charlatan," Glaser said. "And a just bombastic, intimidating, but pretty nice guy. I mean, he was nice to *me*. He was always entertaining. And I kind of wanted to be seen by him, but also, at the same time, wanted him to never know who I was at all—and I wanted no attention from him. Once he liked you, it was, like, too much."

In the 2016 video, Craig described Glaser as "very handsome" before showing a promotional photo she'd signed for the club that reads, "Stanford's—Thanks for giving me my start. I hope Craig never stops hitting on me." And after setting the frame down, Craig added, "I really wanted to mess with her, because she had the same last name. She had a great body. And we hung out and, to be honest, we never slept together."

The video is part of a pretty bizarre web series called *A Man & His Dog*, where Craig—in his sixties with a full head of dyed black hair—would tell implausible stories of his own sexual conquests (sometimes referring to women as "bims," the abbreviated version of "bimbos"), while holding a small dog or two. The videos were lampooned on multiple episodes of *The Bonfire with Big Jay Oakerson and Dan Soder* on SiriusXM, also in 2016. And pretty rightfully so. While I cringed watching Craig display the signed photo of Glaser, assuming she must have put up with a lot of awful shit back then, his comments about

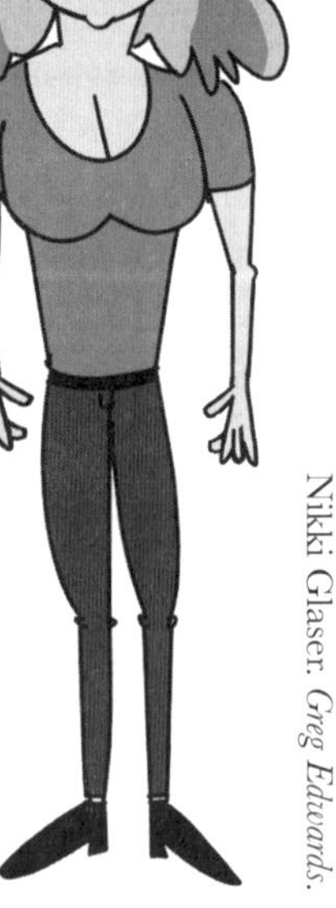

Nikki Glaser. *Greg Edwards.*

her were actually pretty tame compared to things he said in other episodes. And in 2024, Nikki seemed unaffected by all of it.

"He'd say creepy things to me here and there, but I never felt unsafe around him," she said. "I felt objectified and I felt gross sometimes, the way he would leer or look at me or say things. But I didn't really take him seriously, and I never felt victimized by him at all. He was kind of just a ridiculous person that I quickly learned to avoid if I could. But if I couldn't, then I would just laugh at the experience of being around him."

Then, reflecting a little more, she said, "Even me signing that [photo] is, like, rewarding his lascivious behavior. It was me making light of it, which I'm still doing to this day, clearly. Yeah, I was probably still trying to kiss his ass while telling him he was a creep. And yeah, I've never seen that video, but people have told me about it. I just like the memory I have of him and not the one that exists online that's just deranged. I mean, he's insane. People did not like him. But I always got a kick out of him. It seemed cartoonish to me."

After fielding multiple questions about Craig Glazer and Kyle Parris (a bit of a break from the onslaught of interview questions she'd been getting about Tom Brady, Kim Kardashian and Ben Affleck following the roast), Glaser laughed and said, "What a bizarre place to start doing comedy." But then she conceded, "I do consider myself a Kansas City comic. That's who I auditioned with for *Last Comic Standing*. My first thing on TV was me and a bunch of guys from the scene. [We] rented a van. And it was like, nine of us in this passenger van. And we went up to Chicago to audition for *Last Comic Standing*. And that's when I got on TV the first time."

Nikki Glaser's rise to fame began in Kansas City. And in 2025, the sky is seemingly the limit for her. But despite his infamous open mic story, as well as his own very brief appearance on *Last Comic Standing*, fame has eluded Kyle Parris. And despite being the author of a locally known book and having a reality show pilot filmed by Comedy Central in 2003, fame also eluded Craig Glazer. Not that it stopped him from displaying the rock star lifestyle he always cultivated anyway. "When I was in Westport," he told David Hudnall at *The Pitch*, "I literally couldn't keep up with all the women. I'd be hanging out with Johnny Damon, Joe Montana, Pauly Shore. There were women everywhere. At the end of the night, you end up with one or two of them."[77]

But it wasn't too long after the Comedy Central pilot that Stanford's moved from its Westport location. They'd lost an ongoing battle with the neighbors over what type of crowd the club was attracting. It probably didn't help that gunshots had been fired into the club in late 2002 (with Lewis Black allegedly seated close to where a bullet had struck).[78] And when the club moved out of Westport, it marked the end of a magical era. At least for the comics who weren't dodging bullets.

"There's been four other Stanford & Sons [locations]," comedian Justin Leon said. "The Westport room is where I started, and that was the magical room—to me. And so I'll never take anything away from that part of [the Glazers]. They were dirty. They were racist. They were sexist. They were assholes. They were criminals. They were who they were. But as far as holding a spot for comedy? Man, that room was something special for a very long time."

"There's a lot of comedians that hate—*hate*—Craig Glazer," comedian Steve Kramer said. "And in my opinion, unfairly so. I understand if Craig Glazer booked them but didn't pay them what they felt they were worth. Or shorted them on their check. Or did any of those things. They have a right to be upset. But if you try to say that Craig Glazer is a piece of shit, or he doesn't amount to anything. If you try to belittle the things he has accomplished [or] the mark that he left, then really, it says more about you than it does him."

"Craig died still owing me fifty dollars," Tim Gaither said. "So I guess he got me."

"It's crazy that they all kind of died like *Game of Thrones*, one after the other," Glaser said. "They were everywhere—you couldn't get away from the Glazers. There was too many of them. And then there's none of them. It's very sad. And all tragically."

The family's patriarch, Stanford, died in 2022 at the age of ninety. He outlived all three of his sons. Youngest brother Jack died in a car accident in 2011. Middle brother Jeff died of a brain tumor in 2018. And eldest brother Craig died of leukemia later that same year. And there is a lot more to discuss from the legacy of Craig Glazer, which I'll do in the next chapter. But perhaps the most enduring portrayal of the man, at least up to the time of this writing, is actually an animated short made by Kramer, who was one of the few comics in Craig's inner circle. "When people want me to describe the Glazers," a local journalist told me, "I just send them that YouTube link. This is who they were. Like, all the time."

Kramer had helped shoot and edit various reality show pitches for the Glazers over the years (including the aforementioned *A Man & His Dog* series), but none of them had panned out. But one day he just so happened to be waiting for a check in the Stanford & Sons offices, when he began to watch the brothers interact in their weirdly idiosyncratic ways and felt like he was witnessing exactly what their reality show should have been. "You had Jeff trying to order food in his office," Kramer told me. "And Craig's talking to somebody in Hollywood about *The King of Sting*. But they're both talking so loud…and as they're shouting at each other, Jack is in Craig's office swatting at all of these flies with a fly swatter. And I thought to myself, 'My God, if I would have been filming, I could have sold this.'"

So, to re-create that scene, as well as various other classic Glazer brother moments, Kramer taught himself to animate instead. The results, if you ask anyone who knew these guys at that time, were absolutely fantastic. "That thing was great, man," Tim Gaither agreed. "Steve is one of the most talented people I think I've ever met, as far as the amount of things that guy can do."

Kramer—who also produces music, plays and builds guitars, does more than a hundred celebrity impressions and who knows what all else—seemingly nailed everything in the Stanford's animated short, from the stripper girlfriends to the questionable business practices to the previous crimes of Jeff and Jack and just the basic essence of the club, with all its big personalities and drama. Including the fact that the watermelon-smashing comedian Gallagher really did punch Craig in the face in 2010.[79] The cartoon landed Kramer and his short a spot at the prestigious Just for Laughs festival in Montreal soon after.[80] And it probably also proved that the reality show about the Glazers was a missed opportunity by Comedy Central.

"[Stanford & Sons] doesn't get the props that it deserves because it's in the Midwest," Kramer said. "If that shit had happened in Boston, oh my God, there would probably be a movie about it. If it had happened in LA, they would have already made a movie about it. If it would have happened in New York City, they would have already made a movie about it. [The reason it doesn't have a movie is] because it happened in Kansas City."

While the Glazer family's celebrity status stayed local to Kansas City, moving to a bigger market certainly helped spread the legend of Kyle Parris. He landed in Chicago in 2006, and the 'possum story followed him. That might be because Kansas City comic and 'possum story witness Amie Clark also happened to move to Chicago the same year. And it might also be because, oddly enough, so did the man who wanted to wring Parris's neck right after his set. "As God is my witness," former Stanford's GM Ron Meurrens told me, "me and Kyle ran into each other on the same subway train—on the Red Line—one night. Literally three or four months into [moving to Chicago]. We kinda noticed each other at the same time. We're literally sitting across from each other. And I go, 'Did you bring another 'possum on here?' And he kinda smiled at me. Kyle Parris, of all people in the world, is *right across from me*."

Meurrens seemingly never fully recovered from that fateful night in 2001. "I did open a club of my own in Michigan with a partner for a while," he told me, "and everybody asked if we're gonna do an open mic night. But 90 percent because [of] this story, I never was gonna do an open mic night again."

Maybe that's to be expected. But what you wouldn't necessarily expect from a story like that is for it to spark any lasting friendships. But oddly enough, that's exactly what happened with Parris and Andrea Caspari, whose first open mic was the night of the 'possum. Believe it or not, they are best friends—like, actual *best friends*—twenty-four years later. "Maybe it was because I was so traumatized by that [set]," Caspari laughed. "I was like, 'I have to know what's in this guy's mind.' But I love this man with my whole heart. Like, we say 'I love you' when we say goodbye [on the phone]. He is my best, best friend. It's kind of otherworldly how we started. How do you not bond after that?"

Unlikely friendships aside, Parris has had his ups and downs in the recent years since he moved. He was sleeping on a park bench in the northern Chicago suburb of Evanston from 2018 to 2020. Eventually, a local organization called Connections for the Homeless got him an apartment, where he's remained ever since. Parris seems to be adjusting to his new living situation, and he's written multiple episodes of a sitcom based on his experiences on the streets, which he's sent out to various contacts in the industry. And even though it's been more than two decades since that wild night at Stanford's, and even though he's currently living five hundred miles away from where it all went down, Parris is still regularly fielding questions about that infamous set. According to Parris, "Comics are like, 'Dude, tell me the story about the 'possum. I've gotta hear that story.'"

I was obviously one of those comics. And, like me, sometimes comics know the basic details already. Sometimes the story has taken on a life of its own due to an ongoing game of comedian telephone. "I've heard people say, 'Oh, I heard you brought up, like, ten dead armadillos onstage,'" Parris said. "Like, '*What*?'" But the story has stayed alive. And so has the legend of Kyle Parris.

"I feel like there were a thousand rumors about him," Chicago scene veteran Sean Flannery told me about Parris's time there. "The main thing I remember about Kyle Parris is how weird he was considered. Which, in a group as motley and already strange as Chicago stand-up comics, is a unique

Top: Andrea Caspari in a recent image. *Andrea Caspari.*

Bottom: Tom Becka in a recent image. *Tom Becka.*

achievement. The guy was kind of like the hero in a Bob Dylan song, where he was right in front of us the whole time, but nobody knew anything other than rumors about him."

For the comics in Kansas City who witnessed his most infamous set—and I'm talking about the comics, not audience members or the general

Kyle Parris in a recent image. *Kyle Parris*.

manager—there seems to be a true delight in the retelling of this story. And time really does seem to have healed all wounds. "I probably look back on it a little more fondly than I would at the time," Tom Becka said, before conceding, "It was a hell of a night."

"If it weren't for the odor, I think that bit kills." Chris Porter insisted. "It was like when your friend farts, where you're like, 'Goddammit.' Like, it's still *funny*. But it sucks."

"You know," Glaser said, "we're still talking about it. So obviously there was some kind of entertainment value to it."

"At the end of the day," Parris told me, "even though I made people sick, it was in the process of doing something to enlighten them, to liven up their days." Then he paused to consider and took a second crack at it. "I did it mostly for me, to be honest," he said. "I would never do that now."

Chapter 8

THE KING

This all started with a dead 'possum. But it escalated quickly from there. And while I had only been searching for the most infamous open mic story of all time, I accidentally landed on the most infamous modern comedy club, run by the most infamous comedy family in recent memory. And then it got weird.

When I decided to listen to a free download of Craig Glazer's memoir, *The King of Sting*, in May 2024, I'd already been doing interviews that chronicled Craig and Stanford & Sons, so I was invested and felt curious. And I liked the book. It was a pretty fascinating listen. But then, to my utter fucking astonishment, two days after I finished it, I was scrolling through *Deadline* and saw the headline[81] "Eran Creevy to Write & Direct 'The King of Sting.'"

I don't know what the odds could be for a free Audible download from 2008 to be getting any headlines in 2024 at all, let alone days after I completed it, but it still boggles my mind. Especially considering the long and winding road this script has been on since 1981. "Eddie Murphy was attached at one point," Creevy told me when I interviewed him shortly after I read the *Deadline* piece. "I think like, even Nick Nolte back in the '80s. There's been talks of Kurt Russell. Clint Eastwood's production company [Malpaso Productions] had the script for a bit. The guy that directed *Trouble with the Curve* [Robert Lorenz] was attached. The director who wrote *Hurricane* with Denzel Washington and *Wyatt Earp* with Kevin Costner [Dan Gordon] wrote a draft of the screenplay....I think there's been all these amazing incarnations that have existed for the last [41] years."

In *The King of Sting*, Craig also mentions versions of the script written by Nicholas Kazan (son of famed director Elia and writer of *Reversal of Fortune*), Robert Roy Pool (*Outbreak*, *Armageddon*) and even Craig himself. Producer Chuck Roven (*The Dark Knight*, *American Hustle*, *Oppenheimer*) was supposedly attached at one point. And Craig also claimed that there was interest from Walter Hill (*The Warriors*, *48 Hrs.*) and talks of Tom Hanks, Jeff Bridges and Harrison Ford to play either Craig or Don Woodbeck.

With the benefit of time, Creevy's version wound up being different from the others because he decided to ground it in the 2010s, when Craig was the blowhard owner of a comedy club, not just the college-age Robin Hood of the previous scripts. Creevy wanted the trash-talking Stanford & Sons version of Craig to retell his own story—the one who would brag to a journalist about his celebrity pals and sexual conquests. "I was so fascinated, like you are, by the modern-day Craig Glazer," Creevy told me. "I was like, 'This is your key in. This is your point of view on the story. This man. This fucking braggart blowhard bullshitter who is strangely charismatic, strangely hilarious—he's our key into this story.' He's the one who should take us down the rabbit hole. You don't know whether what you're being told is true, but you enjoy the journey nonetheless."

Creevy got his idea when he read a 2013 article in the *Kansas City Pitch* by journalist David Hudnall titled "Craig Glazer Has Lived the American Dream. Are You Listening, Hollywood?" "Glazer was sitting in his cluttered, unglamorous office at Stanford & Sons, the Legends-area comedy club that he owns," Hudnall wrote.[82] "He had been talking, as he often does, about *The King of Sting*.... Turning the story into a movie is a goal that has occupied him on and off since sometime in the 1980s. Now, as he enters his twilight years—he's 60—it has become his dominating passion. He believes that such a movie would corroborate his long-held core belief: that he is a legendary rogue who deserves to be more famous."

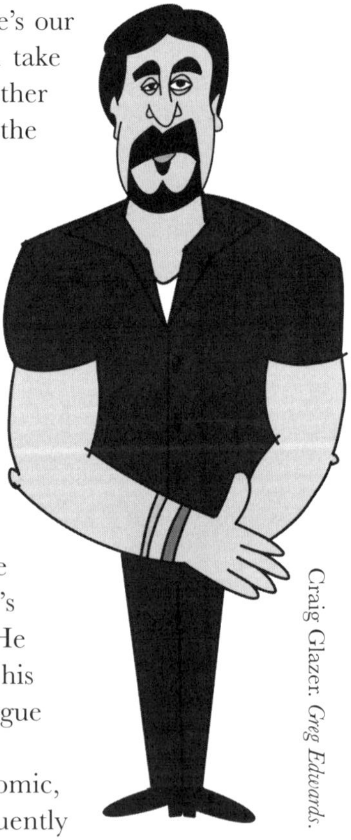

Craig Glazer. *Greg Edwards.*

In the article, where he plays a semi-comic, semi-tragic figure, Craig's interview was frequently interrupted by his brother Jeff, who kept telling him that one of Craig's ex-girlfriends was causing problems in the club. "Get her out of here," Jeff pleaded at one point as Craig was on a tangent about how he launched the careers of Larry the Cable Guy and Lewis Black—or maybe he was on another tangent about which actor from *Twilight* should play him in the movie. "In the middle of this interview," Creevy said, "his brother Jeff comes storming in and goes, 'Get her the fuck out of here. She's been flicking cigarettes at some fucking bim[83] out in the [showroom].' And then [Craig] gets into this big argument with Jeff and with the girlfriend that has come storming in. And I was like, '*That's* my fucking movie. That's the movie—this guy here. This guy in 2013. This fucking character. This iconic arrogant braggart.' He's obsessed with being remembered as an outlaw, [and with] the mythology of what he's trying to build."

It's often hard to separate Craig's mythology-building from the actual facts. I often had to second-guess or even unlearn certain things about the Kansas City comedy scene that I had initially taken at face value before I knew this about him. In other words, Craig was full of shit. He was totally and completely full of shit. To the point that Creevy's *King of Sting* script (or at least the draft that I read) begins with a bit of a disclaimer: "The following is a true story. We think." And sure, Craig didn't necessarily launch the careers of Larry the Cable Guy or Lewis Black. Just like he didn't necessarily launch the careers of Robin Williams or Roseanne Barr or Sinbad or Eddie Griffin. Just like Craig didn't necessarily feud with Griffin. And Griffin didn't necessarily work at the club as a busboy, which was another often-repeated claim. And so on and so forth. As Creevy put it, "The problem is, when you read the book you also go, 'Is this bullshit? Like, is any of this fucking real? Did any of this happen?'"

When I brought up the book to Nikki Glaser, who knew Craig and also read the book, her first response was also to ask me, "Is it all bullshit?"

And it's a valid question. Craig was obviously a truth-stretcher and embellisher about so many parts of his life. And even in his death, he told friends that he had pneumonia when he actually had leukemia. And yes, so much of his time as the "King of Sting" is unprovable anyway. But I still wanted to know if the people who knew him from Stanford & Sons believed his drug world Robin Hood story to be true. Do they believe he set out on a quest for revenge against a dealer and completed thirty-three fake sting operations with guys named Don Woodbeck and Milwaukee Jim? Or is it all bullshit?

"I mean, I remember reading it and feeling like, 'Okay, this probably *did* happen.'" Glaser said. "Why not? He is a guy that just makes shit happen—and seems like such a criminal too. This seems fitting of his character. And like, what would be the point for him [to lie]? He's not a creative person, really. So to me, making all that up seems a little bit out of his wheelhouse, in terms of what he's capable of concocting. So it fits with his character as a criminal. Like, I believed it."

"People make some really poor decisions," former Stanford's bartender Keith Ranney said. "And that sounds like something that he would try to do."

"He'd do anything to get attention," David Naster said. "Anything. And that, to me, was part of his charm."

"I tried to read his book—and I like to read," Tim Gaither told me. "And I got about halfway through that thing and I was like, 'This is such bullshit. There's no way this stuff happened. At least not to this extent.'"

"I don't remember what I thought," comedian Emery Emery responded. "But I do remember what was said after he would finish talking his bullshit. And that is, everybody would go, 'Man, that cokehead is full of shit.' That's the most common reaction when Craig would walk away from whatever bullshit court he was holding. So it didn't take long to figure out that anything Craig said was to be taken with a grain of cocaine."

"He talked about it all the time, but he was such an unbelievable liar," comedian Elliott Threatt said. "One thing's for sure, he was an amazing storyteller and he embellished about *you*. When you were there, he talked about you so much that you felt better about yourself, because he was making you feel better than you ever were. 'Oh, Elliott, you did this. You did that.' And it's like, 'Yeah, I guess I did. I don't remember it that way.' But he made me sound so good when he was doing it that I liked the way he was talking about it."

"Who knows if he did it," Naster said. "I met Woodbeck maybe once or twice. Oh, man. There's something dark there. As they say here in the Midwest, 'Somethin' not right about that boy.' There was something about Woodbeck, when I saw him, that my intuition told me to stay away from this guy."

There's no real way around *that*, I suppose. Craig may or may not have been full of shit, but his partner in crime, Don Woodbeck, was certainly the real deal. And an *Arizona Republic* headline[84] from 1972 shows that a nineteen-year-old Craig was arrested with Woodbeck after a raid by Department of Public Safety agents, who seized sixty-five pounds of marijuana from them. And after Woodbeck and Craig went their separate ways the first time,

Woodbeck began transporting hundreds of pounds of pot from plantations in Mexico across the border into the deserts of Arizona and California via small single-engine planes. According to Craig, "The operation became so well known that it was proudly dubbed the Marijuana Air Force by *High Times* magazine."

This particular squadron of the MAF didn't last long. In October 1977, after a five-month investigation, Woodbeck attempted to evade DEA agents, as well as sheriff's deputies from San Bernardino and Ventura Counties, in a getaway plane after they confiscated six hundred pounds ($90,000 in 1977 money) of marijuana[85] from his drug smuggling operation.

Woodbeck, along with a pilot and his other longtime partner in crime/old Vietnam veteran buddy, "Milwaukee Jim" Wojt, were trying to flee to the Mexican border in a small Beechcraft plane, while authorities pursued them the in the air via helicopters and their own fixed-wing planes. While in the air, agents even fired at Woodbeck's plane with a shotgun in order to ground him. According to Lieutenant James Ferranato of San Bernardino Sheriff's Department Narcotics Office, there were two different times Woodbeck's plane made "threatening moves toward the authorities' aircraft," which warranted the shots. As in, this was a full-fledged dogfight with Woodbeck's pilot attempting to ram a government plane with the Beechcraft at one point and then clip the tail rotor of a helicopter at another. All while the men were seen furiously dumping white envelopes, believed to be four to five pounds of cocaine, out of the aircraft.

So no, Don Woodbeck doesn't seem like the type who would have to lie about his criminal résumé. Then there was obviously his violent death in 1982. You can't really fake that either. As I mentioned earlier, death is not performance. Death is death. Even so, earlier that year, writer Vernon Scott from the *San Pedro News-Pilot* had called[86] Craig and Woodbeck's claims of thirty-three drug robberies "wildly improbable" and added "how much of their story may be unadulterated poppycock apparently doesn't bother CBS Theatrical Films." But shit was about to get very real, very fast—and possibly due to that very article, if you believe Craig's memoir.

According to Craig, Milwaukee Jim was in need of money and knew of a coke dealer being supplied straight from a Colombian cartel. So the plan was to set this guy up for a high-dollar robbery. It would turn out to be the final sting. The dealer's name was Mark Armantrout. And Craig, his cousin Keith, Woodbeck and Milwaukee Jim met with Armantrout at his apartment on the Esplanade in Redondo Beach the night before the murders—ostensibly just to party. Craig knew, though, that Woodbeck and Milwaukee Jim fully intended to rob Armantrout the next day.

Craig would later insist that he and Woodbeck's girlfriend, Debbie, had gone to Woodbeck and Milwaukee Jim's motel in Redondo Beach to try to talk them out of the operation. And in *The King of Sting*, Craig wrote that on the day of the murders, Woodbeck had promised that he was just going to stop by Armantrout's apartment on a social call and not actually go through with the sting. Satisfied with that answer, Craig said he left with Debbie. "Suddenly she had a brainstorm," Craig wrote. Now Debbie wanted a gram of cocaine from Armantrout, so they decided to head back.

"When we returned, there were a half dozen Latinos around [Woodbeck's] El Camino," Craig wrote before adding, "They didn't look like car buffs to me."

According to Craig, he then rushed back up to Armantrout's apartment to warn Woodbeck about the Colombians. And that's when he heard a scuffle from inside the apartment. "An instant later," Craig wrote, "two Latinos crashed through the apartment's window screen and landed on the floor." Then the shooting started.

"POP! POP-POP! POP-POP-POP!" Craig wrote. "One of the Latinos jumped over the railing and hit the concrete ten feet below. The other ran full-speed in the opposite direction from me." In his memoir, Craig said that he assumed it was Woodbeck who was doing the shooting.

Craig also wrote what he believed happened that day, "based on police accounts and court testimony," was that Woodbeck and Milwaukee Jim told Armantrout they wanted to purchase eight ounces of cocaine and were going to spend $20,000 for it. But shortly after entering his apartment, Woodbeck and Milwaukee Jim drew weapons on Armantrout. The Latinos who jumped through the window, Craig believed, were Colombian "cocaine delivery boys." Armantrout tried to put up a fight, so Woodbeck and Milwaukee Jim gave him a beating. Then they cuffed a bloody and beaten Armantrout to his ten-speed bike by the wrist[87] and went about their robbery. It would end up being a fatal mistake.

As Woodbeck and Milwaukee Jim frantically searched the apartment for more cash and more coke, Armantrout pulled an M1 semi-automatic rifle out of his bedroom closet and began firing at his assailants. Woodbeck took four shots to the back. Milwaukee Jim took six. And then Armantrout, who was still handcuffed to his bicycle, "dragged their bodies to the bathroom, put them in the tub, and turned on the water," Craig wrote. "Woodbeck didn't die right away. He bled for a good while first. He was a fighter. He wasn't the kind of guy who would just let go."

Armantrout was charged with two counts of murder soon after. He claimed self-defense. And in 1984, a jury found him not guilty of the murders but guilty of possessing cocaine with intent to sell.[88] A fair deal, I suppose. So was Craig getting immunity from prosecution in exchange for his testimony. And since the highly publicized sting operations of Craig and Woodbeck were crucial to Armantrout's defense, Craig repeatedly denied that Woodbeck had been attempting a sting this time around. Even though he did admit to robbing three cocaine and marijuana dealers earlier in the year.[89] Hilariously, according to the *Redondo Reflex*, "when asked whether he used cocaine the weekend of Woodbeck's death, Glazer said he simulated its use for sting operations" and that he "usually pretended to take cocaine." In other words, he didn't nasally inhale.

Craig's witness credibility was obviously a concern for the defense. Armantrout's lawyers told reporters that Craig might be using the witness stand to perpetuate his own story to sell his movie. But Craig eventually caved under intense questioning. The defense lawyers had gotten to Craig's cousin Keith, who was willing to take the witness stand[90] and contradict his story. And so Craig recanted his previous testimony and admitted to knowing at least a day before the shooting that Woodbeck might be trying to set Armantrout up.

That's about when Craig Glazer lost his heroic stature among the press. Even in their coverage of the murder trial, where the victims of said murder were killed in an attempted sting operation, the *L.A. Times* wrote, "Whether the story [of the previous stings] was real or invented was impossible to tell. Numerous drug officials in Arizona acknowledged that in the early 1970s, several rings engaged in the kind of rip-offs and double-crosses that Glazer and Woodbeck described. But none of the officials remembered the two men's names."

After Craig's testimony, the *Times* wrote that "the image of two tough, loyal buddies" had now been "shattered." When he was "standing outside the apartment in which his associate was about to die," they reminded readers, Craig heard the sounds of a struggle. And when prosecutors had asked Craig what he did next upon hearing those sounds, he told the court he walked back to the elevator and hit the down button. The gunshots started, he told them, right as the elevator door opened. And when another attorney asked Craig why he didn't go back to help his friend, he replied, "You want me to get shot?" As the *Times* put it, "It was a far cry from the heroic tale the two men had told when they hit Los Angeles."

"I think he literally made life choices because he thought, 'Oh, this would be a good thing to happen in a film,'" Creevy said. "He wants to be a modern-day all-American outlaw. He wants to be famous. He wants to be Butch Cassidy and the Sundance Kid. He wants to be Wyatt Earp at the OK Corral....Everything is a reference to it being like a western or the Wild West, and these characters being cowboys, and him being immortalized on the silver screen like these cowboys were. He's just fucking a fascinating character. And whether or not he's a bullshitter, I do think that he did a lot of the stuff."

I suppose I do too. But I also think Craig's desire to get his movie produced outweighed his desire to heroically save his partner in that moment. And I think he knew getting involved in a shootout or a murder could compromise the whole thing—in more ways than one. And in being so close to getting what he wanted, that was not a risk he felt was worth taking. To paraphrase Butch Cassidy, this was no time for bravery. But he probably also knew he couldn't ever admit that to the press.

At the end of the day, or the end of his life, the stuff Craig Glazer did was impressive enough without all the hyperbole. Maybe he wasn't a Robin Hood figure. But he did eventually run Kansas City's first comedy club, which featured legends like Roseanne Barr, Jerry Seinfeld, Robin Williams, Bill Hicks, Sam Kinison and Louie Anderson. His club saw the earliest sets from Sinbad, Eddie Griffin and Nikki Glaser. The Westport location was considered one of the greatest performance spaces in comedy by basically everyone who ever performed there, in spite of how they felt about him personally. And I don't know if I mentioned this yet, but it also saw the most infamous open mic set in the fucking history of comedy.

All of that would have been noteworthy enough. I mean, club owners like Mitzi Shore, Budd Friedman and Jamie Masada are or were pretty renowned in Los Angeles, and none of them ever got into gunfights with Colombian drug cartels. But on top of all that, Craig was an undercover agent for one of the most controversial state attorneys general in the history of this country. He also rubbed elbows with celebrities in Hollywood. And yeah, I think he also probably pulled a few illegal sting operations with Don Woodbeck back in the 1970s and '80s. Maybe he wasn't always the best guy, but Craig Glazer lived a full, interesting, influential life. He is, in all actuality, a legendary rogue who deserves to be more famous. He also happened to be a huge fucking liar. But anti-heroes do make pretty compelling movie characters.

"If I could just walk onto the set of *The King of Sting*, if we could just get that movie made, I could lay down and go to sleep and never wake up after that," Craig told the *Kansas City Pitch* in 2013. "The movie is all that's left for me. Because I've already done everything else. I've been a gunfighter, I've been a special agent, I've been in jail, I've been on the front page, I've slept with all the women, I've hung with the celebrities, I've written a book, I've had a nightclub, I've got the top comedy club."

Nightclub owners from previous eras might have done wilder things like, say, fixing the 1919 World Series or getting JFK elected. But nobody else in the recent history of comedy, and nobody in comedy outside of the mob, has a résumé quite like Craig's. But maybe he wasn't necessarily the best salesman for himself toward the end. "He had written a movie that he was having trouble selling," comedian Dean Boese told me, "but because he knew a lot of people in Hollywood, he would call all the time and try to get it to this person or that person. But the thing was, the comics who would leave Kansas City and go to L.A. would meet these guys. And they would talk to these agents and hear these agents say things like, 'Hey, leave me alone or I'm gonna tell Craig Glazer you're interested in his book.' He was a figure they used to threaten other agents."

"They were probably waiting [to make the movie] until he died or something," comedian Tim Gaither said, "so he wouldn't sit in on the meetings. Because he would have been so annoying about it. Like, 'Well you didn't do that right. That's not true.'"

"I think the movie didn't happen because of Craig," Creevy agreed. "He would be trying to control it too much. And weirdly, his death is what unlocked it all. And it was only by his death that I think the film can now happen...the tragedy of his death and never seeing it happen is kind of what the film is about."

In the 2013 David Hudnall article, Craig was on Johnny Dare's morning radio show with comedian Nick Vatterott when things got testy between Craig and Dare. Dare went for the jugular. "You are going to be the guy whose greatest regret in life is that you didn't get your movie, about you, made," Dare told him. "You know you're never going to get this movie made."

The insult cut Craig deep. "In the parking lot afterward," Hudnall wrote, "Glazer said, 'Look, credit to Johnny: he's the most successful media personality in the history of the city. But is he a friend?' He paused and let a wounded look register briefly on his face. 'You know, would a friend say that he hopes your movie never gets made?'"

"He had a sweetness to him," another local journalist said of Craig. "And kind of a vulnerability to him. Even with all the craziness."

"I could sympathize with him, and I'm sure you can," Creevy said. "We all have these dreams and these aspirations to become famous at what we do. Whether it's being in comedy or whether it's being filmmakers, whether it's being artists or creatives. And he wanted more than anything to see *The King of Sting* come to life. That's all he wants to do. His final goal was to get that movie made. And there was a deep tragedy when I realized that he died in 2018. I thought, 'Fuck, man.'"

"Wow. That makes me so sad that he never got to see that," Nikki Glaser agreed when she heard about the *Deadline* article. "Dude, that was all he talked about. And now it's being made by someone that reputable? Like, *fuck*!"

"Craig always wanted to be a big deal," a local journalist told me. "Especially in Hollywood. Hearing that this is going to become a movie just kinda does my heart good, because I know it would make him so happy."

"That would have been his crowning [achievement]," Gaither agreed. "He was always talking about that."

"I am sad that just a few years after Craig's passing the Chiefs have won three Super Bowls and his movie is going to be made," Steve Kramer said. "Like, the two things that meant the most to him. I would love to have shared that with him."

"He never got to see me kill it at the roast," Glaser added. "Like, he really would have been proud of me. He believed in me before anyone else did. He was a part of my story. I think I would have had the same career without him, but he was the first person to like, throw me into something that I wasn't ready for before anyone. And then I think he was probably the reason I started even working at the club. [He] saw me at an open mic and gave me my first weekends there. Yeah, he was there at the beginning. That's so fucking sad. But so cool that they're making it."

"If nothing else," Craig told Hudnall in 2013, "I'd rather be dead and famous than dead and forgotten."

We all want to be somebody. That was true for Craig. It's true for Eran Creevy. It's true for Nikki Glaser. It's true for Kyle Parris. And it's true for the rest of the comics from this scene. And maybe now it's time they can be, collectively and individually. At the beginning of this book, I wrote that it felt like the universe was telling me to go deeper down this rabbit hole. If I believed in ghosts, I might even think it was Craig himself trying to nudge me along in order to settle unfinished business from beyond the grave.

As Creevy said, Craig's death may have unlocked the movie. But his life also unlocked this book because Kyle Parris may have performed the most infamous open mic set of all time. But the fact that he did it at Stanford & Sons in Westport, and the fact that the club was owned and operated by the King of Sting, means we no longer have to qualify it or limit it to open mics. Now we have the answer to the question I posed at the beginning of the book.

Kyle Parris's set was intentional. And pre-planned. It has its proponents, and it definitely has its detractors. And it's still completely fucking terrifying twenty-four years after it happened. This one holds up. And it takes the cake. Then it strips down to women's underwear and jumps into that cake from high off a stool. Kyle Parris, I can officially declare, has the most infamous stand-up set in the history of comedy.

We may have started with a dead 'possum. But what we wound up with was a GOAT.

ACKNOWLEDGEMENTS

Once again, I would like to thank everyone who took the time to do an interview with me. I especially want to thank Andrea Caspari for getting the ball rolling on this whole thing—and continuing to help throughout. I don't think I could have done this without you.

Thank you to Andrea, Nikki Glaser, William Peck, AJ Finney, Mike Baldwin, Ron Meurrens, Elliott Threatt, Tom Becka, Maureen Bridenstine, David Naster, Amie Clark, Tim Gaither, Jeff Johnson, the Missouri Valley Special Collections, David Hotle from the *Muscatine Journal* and Kyle Parris for providing photos.

Thank you to Nikki, Tom Segura, Eric Andre, Kyle Kinane, Kyle Ayers, Brooks Wheelan, Eran Creevy and Rory Scovel for the nice quotes.

Thank you to the Kansas City comedy scene for allowing me into its world. I just hope I got it right.

Thank you to David Naster for having me on his podcast and also helping throughout. You're a legend, brother.

Thank you to Chris Porter for the foreword.

Thank you to Andrea, Philip Hollingsworth and especially Robert Buscemi for editorial guidance.

Thank you to Greg Edwards and Jake Lloyd Bacon for the cover art. And to Greg for the illustrations.

Thank you to Joe Gartrell and everyone at The History Press.

Thank you to my family for their love and support.

Thank you to Jason Zinoman, *YHM*, the Lincoln Lodge, Steve Heisler, Rebecca George, Volumes Bookcafe, Nate Craig, *ChicagoMag*, Kelly Leonard, Teme Ring, Carl Kozlowski, WGN, Alison Rosen, *Dumb People Town*, *Jordan Jesse Go*, the Art Institute of Chicago, the *Hunk* listeners and all the people who bought my last book. You all made me think I could do another one.

Thank you to Sean Casey, Anne Gregory, Jake Kroeger, Uriah Wesman and everyone at the Lyric Hyperion.

Thank you to Thom Sigsby, Danny Ledsinger, Kevin Silva, David Jackson, Damu Malik and the whole Microdose/Fable family.

Thank you to Victoria and Taker—for continuing to be my "why."

NOTES

Foreword

1. This was Craig Glazer's catchphrase.

Prologue

2. I know it happened by October 1990 because it was referenced in an article in the *Abilene (TX) Report-News* from October 12, 1990.
3. Cooper also happens to be the inspiration for the fezzes worn at the Lincoln Lodge in Chicago since 2000.
4. Rod McPhee, "Tommy Cooper's Dark Side: 'I'd See Bruises on My Mum…He Threw Her Across a Room,'" *Irish Mirror*, April 19, 2014.
5. "Actor and Workman Killed, 8 Hurt in Crash at Muehlebach Hotel," *Kansas City Post*, December 28, 1914, 1.
6. "A Third Collapse Victim," *Kansas City Times*, December 29, 1914, 2.
7. Klipf Nesteroff, *The Comedians* (Grove Press, 2015).
8. Forrest Duke, "Aladdin Snuffs Its Pryor Lamp," *Arizona Republic*, October 11, 1967, 45.
9. *Muhammad Ali*, directed by Ken Burns, Sarah Burns and David McMahon, with performances by Keith David, Florentine Films, 2021.

Introduction

10. Mike Hlas, "The Night Norm Macdonald Mortified the University of Iowa," *Cedar Rapids Gazette*, June 21, 2017.
11. "No Laughing Matter for Iowa," *Muscatine Journal*, June 24, 1997, 11.
12. For the record, a member of the improv troupe told me that they only did a twenty-minute set that night. He was also *definitely* not a fan of Macdonald's performance later in the show.
13. David Lee, "'SNL' Trio Brings Act to Hancher," *Iowa City Press-Citizen*, June 21, 1997, 17.
14. Linda Huang-Eans, "Bowlsby Apologizes for Comedian's Remarks," *Iowa City Press-Citizen*, June 24, 1997, 3.
15. Charles Bullard, "Raunchy Routine Draws Apology," *Des Moines Register*, June 24, 1997, 1.
16. John Kenyon, "Athletics Officials at U of I Issue Apology for Comedian," *Cedar Rapids Gazette*, June 24, 1997, 11.
17. "Norm MacDonald [*sic*] Gets Kicked Out of Iowa," Jim Breuer's Breuniverse, uploaded November 10, 2010, via YouTube, https://www.youtube.com/watch?v=gBKlXR3BbDU.
18. "Norm Macdonald Stand Up—Similar to the 1997 Iowa Routine," Norm's Stand Up Vault, uploaded November 26, 2021, via YouTube, https://www.youtube.com/watch?v=m2xng3uSNUQ&t=1s.
19. John Kenyon, "Comedians Varied Laughs at 'Live From Iowa City' Show," *Cedar Rapids Gazette*, June 24, 1997, 11.
20. "Stern—Norm MacDonald Calls in [June 27, 1997]," uploaded by Henryk Szlangbaum, August 3, 2013, via YouTube, https://www.youtube.com/watch?v=wbDGCoM2Flw.
21. David Wild, "Looking for the Heart of 'Saturday Night,'" *Rolling Stone* (November 27, 1997).
22. John Kenyon, "U of I Letter on Comedian's Wall," *Cedar Rapids Gazette*, November 15, 1997, 11.

Chapter 1

23. I believe this happened on *Open Mike with Mike Bullard* on February 12, 1998.
24. Blake Burkhart and James Webb, "The Legend of Kyle Parris," *Chicago Comedy Show*, July 6, 2021.

25. Jeff Strait, "Funny Farm," *Kansas City Star*, December 31, 2005, 166.

Chapter 2

26. Brad Austin, "What Are the 3 Oldest Buildings in KC?" Flatland KC, March 5, 2019.
27. Craig Glazer, *The King of Sting* (Skyhorse Publishing, 2008).
28. Christopher Hearne Jr., "Last Laugh?: Glazer Pops Pop's Balloon," *Kansas City Star*, July 9, 2008, 49.
29. Joyce Smith, "Landlord Suing Stanford & Sons," *Kansas City Star*, February 10, 2001, 25.
30. Jeffrey Spivak and Joyce Smith, "For the Kings of Comedy, a Tragedy Is Playing Out," *Kansas City Star*, November 26, 2000, 20.
31. Tim Engle, "Craig Glazer Rats Himself Out," *Kansas City Star*, July 6, 2008, G9.
32. "Stanford and Sons Cartoon Pilot," uploaded by Steve Kramer, April 18, 2012, via YouTube, https://www.youtube.com/watch?v=FJ7s18fHk7Y.
33. Peter H. Brown, "Kansas City Controversy: Drug Buy Staged for TV," *Los Angeles Times*, July 5, 1981, 207.
34. In his book, Craig says that his classmates included Tom Selleck and Lou Ferrigno.
35. Doug Smith, "Drug 'Vigilantes' Leave Murky Trail," *Los Angeles Times*, October 6, 1982, 30.
36. Dan Weikel, "Final Sting May Have Led to Redondo Slayings," *Daily Breeze* (Torrance, CA), August 29, 1982, 1.
37. Ray Morgan, "Miller, Drug Official Differ on Glazer Topic," *Kansas City Times*, July 4, 1974, 4.
38. Lew Ferguson, "Kansas' Precedent-Defying Attorney General Becomes a Big Name in the State," *Long Beach Independent*, March 25, 1971, 81.
39. James A. Kidney, "Vern Miller Voted Kansas' Top Newsmaker," *Wichita Eagle*, December 24, 1971, 11.
40. John Petterson, "Docking Eyes Coattails of Miller," *Wichita Eagle*, August 1, 1971, 16.
41. Amy Renee Leiker, "Legendary Kansas Lawman Vern Miller Dies at 92," *Wichita Eagle*, June 13, 2021, A1.
42. "No Rolling Saloons in Kansas," *Kansas City Star*, July 24, 1972, 22.
43. Charles Hillinger, "Super Sherif Puts Sky-High Lid on Kansas," *Los Angeles Times*, March 29, 1973, 110.

44. Roy Wenzl, "Former Drug Case Figure Mellows with the Years," *Kansas City Star*, June 28, 1979, 24.
45. Cathleen Decker and Bill Farr, "Self-Styled Drug Vigilante Gets 7 Years in Prison," *Los Angeles Times*, April 16, 1985, 3.
46. "Former Kansas Agent Guilty in Cocaine Case," *Kansas City Star*, March 7, 1985, 7.

Chapter 3

47. Craig Glazer, "Glazer: KC Comedy Kingpin David Naster Calls It Quits," *KC Confidential*, November 27, 2011.
48. Shifira Stein, "What's a Girl to Do? Listen to Cal Coolidge," *Kansas City Star*, September 8, 1977, 8.
49. Joe Rassenfoss, "Comedian Leaves Fans Laughing," *Kansas City Star*, June 14, 1982, 14.
50. Ward W. Triplett III, "The Serious Business of Making Kansas City Laugh," *Kansas City Star*, June 9, 1991, 184.
51. Brian McTavish, "Popping the Clutch on a Comedy Career," *Kansas City Star*, November 28, 1986, 39.
52. Joyce Eileen Smith, "Stanford & Sons to Open Billiard Hall in Westport," *Kansas City Star*, December 30, 1994, B-2.
53. Mike Saccone actually won *Star Search* in 1989.
54. Craig Glazer, "Glazer: KC Comedy Kingpin David Naster Calls It Quits," *KC Confidential*, November 27, 2011.
55. It gets a little confusing, but from 1980 to May 1986, the club was in the "Tree House" at 504 Westport. Then, due to the construction of the Manor Square complex next door, the shows moved down the street to 543 Westport. And there are show listings there from 1986 to 1987 and then from 1990 to 1996, with some listings for shows at 508 Westport from 1988 to 1990. There was also a second location in Overland Park, Kansas, at 9045 Metcalf from 1989 to 1995 and then at 10635 Floyd (Hooters Plaza) beginning in 2000. And in 2001, the Westport version of the club moved back to its original location at 504 Westport, where it remained until 2004. We'll save the rest of the moves for later in the book.
56. Bob Ivry, "'Foolish' Is the Title Not the Plan," *Kansas City Star*, April 24, 1999, 57.
57. Ward W. Triplett III, "Not Just a Face in the Crowd," *Kansas City Star*, October 30, 1992, 104.

Chapter 4

58. Christopher Hearn Jr., "No Joke: Glazer Serious About Running for Mayor," *Kansas City Star*, March 15, 2001, 50.
59. Lynn Horsley, "Glazer's Statement Rebuts Allegations," *Kansas City Star*, March 8, 2003, 18.
60. Barbara Shelley, "Barnes Deserves New Term," *Kansas City Star*, March 15, 2003, 15.
61. David Hudnall, "Craig Glazer Has Lived the American Dream. Are You Listening, Hollywood?" *The Pitch*, July 4, 2013.

Chapter 5

62. Yes, that's his birth name.
63. Timothy Finn, "If You're Not Offended, Emery Emery Hasn't Done His Job," *Kansas City Star*, November 29, 1996, 123.
64. Stanford University, Stanford Disability, "Disability Language Guide," https://disability.stanford.edu/sites/g/files/sbiybj26391/files/media/file/disability-language-guide-stanford_1.pdf.
65. Chris Fonseca, "Biography," https://www.fonsecacomedy.com/bio.
66. Christopher Hearne Jr., "Cerebral Palsy Isn't Funny…but He Is," *Kansas City Star*, October 23, 1998, 47.
67. "Stargazing," *Kansas City Star*, October 11, 2004, 37.
68. *All Comedy Radio* 1340 KCKN, with Elliott Threatt, Scott Voorhees and A. Whitney Brown, October 25, 2004.

Chapter 6

69. Tim Engle, "Comic 'Survivors' Will Give Audience Last Laugh," *Kansas City Star*, August, 11, 2000, 162.
70. "Episode 9," *On the Record with Bob Costas*, created by Bob Costas, season 3, HBOMax, June 27, 2003.
71. Ward W. Triplet III, "A Sonny Outlook," *Kansas City Star*, July 31, 1996, 52.
72. "Dead Possum Story," uploaded by Janette Perez, June 22, 2014, via YouTube, https://www.youtube.com/watch?v=zFEdSN6FwOQ.

Chapter 7

73. Chris Vognar, "Why Nikki Glaser Is Suddenly the Hottest Name in Comedy," *Los Angeles Times*, August 19, 2024.
74. Tony Maglio, "Netflix's Tom Brady Roast Really Shouldn't Have Been Live," IndieWire, May 6, 2024, https://www.indiewire.com/features/commentary/tom-brady-roast-netflix-kevin-hart-1235000934.
75. Jason Zinoman, "Netflix Gives Comedy the Live Treatment. The Results Are Chaotic," *New York Times*, May 7, 2024; Mike Fleming Jr., "Nikki Glaser Killed It at the Tom Brady Roast with John Wick Efficiency; How the Stage Saved Her Life Literally: The Film that Lit My Fuse," *Deadline*, May 10, 2024.
76. Stanford's Comedy Club, "Craig Glazer, *A Man & His Dog*, Episode 11—Nikki Glaser," August 30, 2016, via YouTube, https://www.youtube.com/watch?v=VKurbdmnrEk&list=PLEAhlA3g9bJkY0h4oeV7jZrTviV_kiAZl&index=1.
77. Hudnall, "Craig Glazer Has Lived the American Dream."
78. Joe Lambe, "State Investigates Comedy Club Shooting," *Kansas City Star*, May 24, 2003.
79. Craig Glazer, "Glazer: Hell Rejects Gallagher After Heart Attack on Stage in Minnesota," *KC Confidential*, March 12, 2011.
80. "Glazers: A Laugh Riot," *Kansas City Star*, July 21, 2012, C4.

Chapter 8

81. Nancy Targalione, "Eran Creevy to Write & Direct 'The King Of Sting'; Silver Reel Financing & Producing—Cannes Market," *Deadline*, May 17, 2024.
82. The Overland Park club moved to Legends Outlets mall in Kansas City, Kansas, in 2007, then to Rosana Square Shopping Center in Overland Park in 2014 and then back to Legends in 2016. There was also a bit of a residency at the Uptown Theater in Kansas City, Missouri, in 2013. But the final location was at 813 Walnut in downtown Kansas City, which was, according to all accounts, a real fall from grace. Two men were even shot and seriously injured inside the location in the wee hours of the morning in February 2018. Craig had told the *Star* that a cleaning crew had been inside at the time of the shooting. But no such cleaning crew existed. In fact, management allegedly called local comedians to help clean the blood

off the floor and hang pictures over the bullet holes in an attempt to have a show the night of.

83. Again, that's Craig-speak for "bimbo," which Creevy and I had both seen him use in a YouTube video to describe a woman.
84. "3 Seized in Marijuana Raid," *Arizona Republic*, December 1, 1972, 4.
85. "Drug Runners Nabbed in Wild Air Chase," *Desert Trail* (Twentynine Palms, CA), October 27, 1977, 1.
86. Vernon Scott, "Glazer, Woodbeck Make Larceny Pay," *News-Pilot* (San Pedro, CA), March 19, 1982, 32.
87. Doug Smith, "Drug Vigilantes Leave Murky Trail," *Los Angeles Times*, October 6, 1982, 30.
88. John Needham, "Pusher Not Guilty of Double Murder," *Los Angeles Times*, May 17, 1984, 22.
89. Dan Weikel, "Murder Victim's Pal Didn't Suspect Sting, Court Told," *Redondo Reflex*, September 22, 1982, 3.
90. Dan Weikel, "Redondo Man Will Face Murder Charge," *Redondo Reflex*, September 29, 1982, 1.

ABOUT THE AUTHOR

Mike Bridenstine is a comedian and author originally from Muscatine, Iowa. He has performed at festivals all around the United States, Canada and the UK, including New Faces at the Just For Laughs Festival in Montreal. Some of his TV credits include *Last Call with Carlson Daly* on NBC, *Adam DeVine's House Party* on Comedy Central, *The Eric Andre Show* on Adult Swim and *High Potential* on ABC. You can listen to his comedy albums *The Hungry Wolf Hunts Best* and *Hustle* from AST Records on Apple and Spotify. His first book, *The Perfect Amount of Wrong*, was called "catnip for comedy nerds" by Jason Zinoman of the *New York Times*. This is his second book.